A QUARTER GLASS OF MILK

THE RAWNESS OF GRIEF AND THE POWER OF THE MOUNTAINS

MOIRE O'SULLIVAN

THE O'BRIEN PRESS
DUBLIN

MOIRE O'SULLIVAN is a mountain runner, adventure racer, author and mum. Her company, Happy Out Adventures, brings people onto the trails and mountain slopes, teaching them how to enjoy the outdoors happily and safely. She is the author of *Mud, Sweat and Tears, Bump, Bike and Baby: Mummy's Gone Adventure Racing* and *The Hound From Hanoi.*

Dedication

To Leona and Julie

For always being there for me and my boys

First published 2021 by The O'Brien Press Ltd,
12 Terenure Road East, Rathgar, Dublin 6, D06 HD27, Ireland.
Tel: +353 1 4923333; Fax: +353 1 4922777
E-mail: books@obrien.ie. Website: www.obrien.ie
The O'Brien Press is a member of Publishing Ireland.

ISBN: 978-1-78849-227-0

8 7 6 5 4 3 2 1
23 22 21

Printed and bound by ScandBook UAB, Litauen.
The paper in this book is produced using pulp from managed forests.

Front cover photograph by Gareth McCormack
Back cover photograph by Quest Ireland
Author photograph p2 by Ian MacLellan

Published in

CONTENTS

CHAPTER 1

LAST YEAR

'I meant to get in touch last year,' he said. 'It's just, I didn't know what to say.'

I froze, people pushing past us on either side. The mere mention of last year pinned me to the ground.

I hadn't seen Eoin in years, even though we had been friends back in the day. I wasn't surprised to see him, however. It was inevitable we were going bump into each other at a gathering such as that evening's.

It was the night of the premiere of *Coming Home*, a film about emigrant and mountain runner Paddy O'Leary returning to Ireland to attempt the Wicklow Round. I too had completed this gruelling challenge. I was the first person to successfully summit the Wicklow Mountains' twenty-six peaks within twenty-four hours. There was no way I was missing the screening of this feat of endurance that had been such an integral part of my own life.

Eoin, too, was a mountain runner, one who had cruised the Wicklow Round on the day of his own attempt. For him it was just one more thing to add to his phenomenal list of athletic achievements.

Over a decade had passed since both Eoin and I had completed our Wicklow Rounds. So much had happened in the intervening years. But 'last year', the time that Eoin spoke of now, well that was different.

'It's okay, don't worry about it,' I replied quickly, swiftly brushing his comment away. Eoin wasn't the only person who had no idea what to say to me. It was kind of him though to bring it up, to acknowledge my terrible loss. I had encountered others who were well aware of what had happened, yet jovially asked whether I was still racing in the mountains when that was the furthest thing from my mind. Eoin was brave enough not to ignore what was foremost in my life.

'It's just that,' Eoin continued, 'I wanted to let you know, my Dad died when I was five.' He then looked me square in the eye and said, 'Your kids will be okay.'

My throat choked hard as he said those final words. Now it was I, not Eoin, who did not know what to say. Here was Eoin, not telling that he was sorry for my loss, or telling me how hard it was going to be. Instead here was Eoin, who had excelled at so much, in a few simple words offering me hope. My boys and I would be okay.

CHAPTER 2

THAT DAY

I looked at the clock. It read 9.45 am. He was late. My husband Pete was never late.

We had planned to visit Pete's sister, two days after Christmas. He had gotten up early that morning, a surprising yet welcome move. We had a long drive ahead of us, at least six hours, so I was looking forward to making the most of the winter's daylight. Even better was the fact that Pete was dressed for a morning run.

'We need to leave at 10 am at the latest,' I told him. 'So if you could be back by 9.30, that would be great.' He nodded slowly, his eyes fixed on the bowl of steaming porridge that I had given him, which he now cradled in one hand. It was still dark outside, but he had his fluorescent vest on, so would be visible on the road.

A run would be good. He had not been well of late, and running was meant to help.

'Why don't you bring Tom?' I asked; our dog instantly jolted his head upright at the mention of his name. Tom was going to be cooped up in the car with us for the long journey, so an early-morning run with his master would do both the world of good.

'No!' Pete replied. I was taken aback. His abrupt reaction didn't make sense. I didn't want to push it, however. The fact that Pete was up, dressed, eating and about to exercise already made it a good day.

I knew Pete's route off by heart. He was a remarkable creature of habit. Turning out of our front drive, he would run down the road for a kilometre before turning left into Kilbroney forest. He would then run up the hill, following the Mourne Way trail until he reached the car park at Yellow River. From there he would run back home via the road to complete his ten-kilometre circuit. It took him an hour, always one hour.

By 9.45 am, an hour fifteen had passed. I was starting to get worried.

Leaving our house, I walked towards the road to see if there were any signs of Pete. As I stood at our gateway, scanning the road to my left and right through the dim December light, my landlord Michael appeared on the other side of the road.

'Have you seen Pete?' I asked, dispensing with pleasantries while trying to maintain a sense of calm. My head was muddled with what could have happened my partner. As he shook his head, I remembered that Michael had a four-wheel drive and keys to the gate that allowed vehicles to enter the forest. 'It's just that, he's late. Could you maybe go see if he's had an accident?' I said. 'He could be injured somewhere on the forest road. It's just…not like him.'

As he returned to his home to gather his keys, I ran back to our house. I knew Pete would kill me for what I'd do next, but I had no other option. Only a few days beforehand, Pete had been discharged from hospital. He had been treated there for depression, before being handed over to a home-based care team. The team had given me their contacts in case of anything. I dialled the number on their card.

'He's gone missing,' I said to the man who answered the phone. 'I know it's probably nothing, but I just thought you should know.' I had convinced myself that Pete had probably gone for a wander up one of the surrounding hills, above the forest tree line. Knowing him, Pete had worked out that if he delayed us by just enough we would be too late to leave that day, and the trip would eventually get called off. Pete didn't like travelling much of late.

I explained that my landlord was currently checking the trail to see if Pete was lying there, injured. 'If he comes back saying there's no sign, call the police,' the man said.

I baulked at the suggestion. If Pete hobbled home only to see police cars parked on our drive, I knew he would lose the plot. Pete had managed thus far to keep news of his illness within close confines. Informing the police was akin to broadcasting it publically on social media.

When Michael returned without Pete in tow, I knew I had little choice. Maybe it would be better if the police got involved and the community came to know that he was not well. Maybe it would be a silver lining.

My 999 call was answered quickly, setting the train in motion. The policeman's questions came thick and fast. What was he wearing? Where was he going? When was he meant to return? Did he have any friends he could be visiting locally? Did he bring his wallet or phone?

I stood outside the house in the winter air as I took the call, hoping I would catch sight of Pete returning from his run. Once I saw him, I planned to hang up as if nothing had happened, so that we could go back to how things were.

The policeman told me that he'd send out a team to help coordinate a search. I'd agreed to whatever was suggested if it meant Pete could come home safely. In the meantime the policeman told me to phone anyone who I thought Pete could have gone and visited. I quickly realised there was no one Pete knew well enough to engage in a social call. We had lived in the village of Rostrevor for over three years, and yet Pete hadn't made friends in the same way I had. He hadn't done the school pick-ups and mingled with parents, or joined the local running groups.

The only person I could think of was John, a former neighbour of ours, but John now lived a thirty-minute drive away over narrow rural roads. There was no way Pete could have run there. Regardless, I dialled John's number and apologised for disturbing him in the midst of the Christmas holidays.

'I know this is a long shot,' I said. 'But is Pete there? It's just that…he's gone missing.'

I still don't recall our conversation, a consequence, I now realise, of my mind drawing a veil across that day. What happened in those next few hours was probably so traumatic that memory failure is the only way to protect me.

A call was then made to Pete's sister who we were meant to visit, to tell her we were delayed. I didn't want to alarm her, as I knew Pete would be home soon, but I just wanted to let her know that our anticipated arrival time of 4 pm was no longer feasible.

A police team soon arrived at the door, two officers, both looking so young. There was part of me that didn't want to distress these millennials with my troubles, when they had surely more pressing things to do. They asked the same questions as the ones I had answered on the phone, and I tried to be consistent and clear. I also gave them a photo of Pete to show to locals during their enquiries in case it helped track him down. My emotions were in check throughout, knowing there was no point in hysterics, because Pete would be home soon.

It was only when John and his wife Nina arrived at my door as the officers were leaving that I realised something was maybe wrong. I hadn't asked them to come. John's eyes were raw and red. What did he know that I didn't?

I had allowed John and Nina into our inner circle many months before. I had told them Pete was unwell, that he needed a bit of help. I had let John know that Pete wasn't answering his phone and had stopped working. John and Nina immediately invited us over for drinks and dinner. They hadn't seen Pete in a couple of weeks, a consequence of his self-enforced isolation. It was obvious that Pete had lost weight, one of the many apparent symptoms of his growing illness.

'Are you on a new diet?' John joked as Pete played around with the chunks of chicken on his plate. Pete would normally wolf down John's excellent cooking. 'Are you going to let us in on your secret?'

This I knew was Pete's chance to say, 'Yeah, I'm not doing too well these days.' Instead Pete nodded quietly. 'Diet…Yeah, that's it,' he mumbled back, avoiding all eye contact.

Before I could say to John that he shouldn't have come, that there was no need for any fuss, John said, 'Hope for the best…but expect the worst.' I was stunned, too shocked to provide a counter argument. John then turned to the police team who were now outside, to help them with their enquiries. Nina slipped into our house, volunteering to stay with me while we waited.

The daughter and wife of my landlord, Didi and Marie, soon came to the house and asked my boys, Aran and Cahal, if they'd like to visit their resident chickens. I hadn't noticed that their childish noises had already faded deep into the background, so distracted had I become. They needed to be looked after by someone who was fully functioning. The chance of feeding chickens seemed to them the opportunity of a lifetime. As they donned their wellies and jackets, Didi suggested she stay behind with Nina and I to help coordinate the search.

Didi, with her extensive contacts throughout the community, was already way ahead of me. She had messaged local mountain bikers and asked them to keep an eye out for Pete if they happened to be out for a spin. Though I knew Pete wouldn't have purposely gone on the forest's mountain bike trails, if he had had a bad fall he could potentially be lying on one, calling out for help.

Didi continued to flick through her long list of friends, trying to think of anyone else who could help.

'Would it be okay if I called Marty, from the Mourne Mountain Rescue Team?' Didi then said. I hesitated, not wanting to bother them. I knew the Mountain Rescue Team is made up purely of volunteers. These men and women were probably looking forward to some downtime after the Christmas rush. The last thing I wanted was for them to abandon their festive plans to trawl the forests and mountains for my missing husband.

It was just that, if Pete was hurt, he needed to get home fast. I was deeply worried that he was cold, tired, hungry, afraid. If someone, anyone could help locate him, I was more than willing to accept their help. I would suffer the consequences later when Pete berated me for overreacting to his absence.

So, Didi called Marty, who immediately agreed to assemble the Mountain Rescue Team. I felt embarrassed yet extremely grateful. She then slipped away to check on my kids and to make sure they were still distracted.

Without my husband or children around, the house was strangely quiet.

Nina and I stood like statues beside the window that overlooked the road, hoping to catch a glimpse of Pete running back up the tarmac.

'Do you want a cup of tea or something?' she asked, trying to break the silence. I shook my head. Drinking tea would sidetrack me from my mission of willing Pete home safely.

'You know, Pete wouldn't hurt himself on purpose,' I said. 'He just wouldn't.' Nina stared blankly back at me. 'I remember talking with Pete once, a long time ago, about suicide. And I remember him telling me how he just couldn't understand why anyone would ever want to do such a thing.'

What I wasn't taking into account was that Pete had been suffering from depression for a while. It meant that the Pete I knew, the one with whom I had had this conversation, that Pete was no longer present.

'And anyhow, he loves the boys too much,' I said. It was like I was trying to convince Nina that her husband John had got it all wrong. I told her of how Pete had recently visited Tim, a good friend of his, whose wife had suddenly passed away at the age of forty-nine. There had been no warning. Medics suggested that it had been a brain aneurism that had taken her peacefully while she slept. I explained to Nina how upset Pete had been when he visited his friend, when he saw how Tim had to bring up three children who were now without their amazing mother. 'Pete would never leave our boys without a father,' I said, not doubting my words for a second. I knew my Pete too well.

My monologue was soon cut short by the sound of a helicopter. Its blades sliced through the air as it raced over our heads towards the adjacent forest.

'It's a heat-seeking helicopter,' Nina quickly explained as we stared at it through the window. I didn't know whether I wanted it to scan the forest, then move quickly away, or for it to hover and zone in on an area. Helicopters only really turned up in these parts when badly injured people were being airlifted to hospital. The idea of Pete being hurt scared me. I watched the helicopter's erratic movements before it finally flew away. I still wasn't sure what was happening.

Soon enough the police team arrived back, asking the same questions as before. 'Did he bring his wallet? Did he leave his phone? Can you describe again what he was wearing?' I poked around in Pete's drawers, pulling out similar items of clothing to give them anything that matched what I had seen him leave in. During my search, I located his wallet, but couldn't trace his mobile. He must have brought it with him.

'Did the helicopter find any sign of Pete?' I asked them when I got a chance, knowing full well that if it had, this would have been the first thing the police would have told me.

'No,' they replied, 'but the Mountain Rescue Team are searching the Mourne Way again, where you think he may have been running. We'll let you know if there are any updates.' Nina told me that John had joined the team, helping them in their efforts. We knew that if there were any updates, he'd quickly let us know.

Just as the police team was leaving, a second police car pulled into the top drive, stopping outside our front gates, blocking our team's exit. 'That's our sergeant,' they informed us. 'If there's any news, he'll have it.'

The sergeant stepped out of his car, looked towards us and tapped his cap firmly twice. I knew it meant something, possibly good news that they'd found him. The two police officers quickly walked towards him, as Nina and I stood back and watched them conversing from afar.

I assumed that they had indeed found Pete, but that he didn't want to come back home. He was probably furious with me that I'd called the police and a helicopter and mountain rescue out, and ruined his tranquil run. Knowing Pete, he would want me to promise to leave him alone until he was feeling better.

So when the sergeant walked towards me and asked me to step into the house, I just wondered what Pete had told him to make him act so officious. Bringing the sergeant into our living room, I sat myself down on the sofa's armrest, ready for him to relay Pete's requests. The sergeant remained standing, close, too close to me. His police officers flanked him on either side. Nina hovered on my left.

'We've found a body.' The words pierced through me, cutting me deep within. The next thing I heard was my desperate primordial scream. There was no way this could be happening.

CHAPTER 3

THAT NIGHT

All I remember is Nina holding me in a vice-like grip as I screamed and screamed and screamed, until I had no more screams left to give.

'We need to formally identify the body,' the sergeant told me once I had quietened down, before quickly informing me that it was most likely Pete. In one fell swoop, the sergeant dispelled any hope I may have had that they had stumbled upon a different casualty.

'Do you want me to… Do you need me to…' I said, trying to step up and do my perceived spousal duty to identify the body.

'No need,' he said. 'John is on site and has offered. We should hear within the hour.' Then he uttered the words that I was to hear *ad nauseam*, 'I'm sorry for your loss.'

I was still in deep denial about Pete's intentions. It must have been an accident, a terrible accident. 'Was it a bad fall?' I asked. I imagined that it was just a moment of thoughtlessness, a last-minute action where Pete had tumbled off one of the river's bridges, killing himself on the jagged boulders that I knew lay beneath.

Finding out that he had hung himself caused my brain to shut down. I couldn't believe Pete had left home with such a deliberate plan. Shock numbed my senses. Suddenly there were people everywhere, standing close, so close. Word had somehow reached the village that a body had been found, and friends had come to help. Only, when they spoke to me, their mouths moved, but their words made no sense. Their hands wiped swiftly beneath bloodshot eyes. They were sorry for my loss. In the blur of people, Pete's brother and his wife arrived at the house to the tragic news.

Fortunately someone thought of my kids, who I had forgotten. I assumed they were still feeding chickens. They told me they would take my children away for the night for a sleepover and bring them back in the morning. It gave me a chance to deal with other more pressing issues like the police and the coroner and a funeral. It also gave me a chance to prepare how I would tell them that Daddy was never coming home again.

Soon enough, the police relayed back to me that the body was indeed Pete's. There was no more hiding from the truth. With the news came John's arrival, looking like a shell of the man that I once knew. I hugged him, knowing what he had done would scar him forever. Pete would never have wanted to cause him such hurt.

Before slipping back to his home with Nina, John issued me with a warning. 'A friend of mine died when I was young,' John told me, trying to remain composed. 'I saw his body lying in his coffin.' He looked straight at me with weary eyes. 'I've always lived to regret it.' I stared back at John, unsure. 'If you see Pete now, remember you'll never un-see him', he said. 'Think carefully about how you want to remember him.' Looking back, I see that John's words were a mere rumble before the avalanche of advice I'd receive after Pete's demise, a landslide that I'd at times feel snowed under. John's suggestion rang true for me right at that moment, though such advice might not have worked for others.

A voice asked me if I wanted the local doctor, Henry, to call up to the house. I agreed, because it seemed the right thing to do. I had spoken to Henry before about Pete, when he was admitted to hospital the previous month. Henry had been honest then. He was known to be pragmatic. Maybe he would tell me what the hell I was meant to do now.

The living room was cleared to let Henry and me sit down in isolation. Condolences were quickly dispensed with.

'Pete could have been ill for years and then done this,' Henry said. 'You mightn't be able to see it now, but Pete wanted the best for you and the boys.' My brow furrowed in disbelief, wondering if this was how you put a positive spin on suicide. The passage of time has since revealed that Henry was indeed correct. Pete's depression had only lasted half a year, so short when compared to those who suffer from it for a lifetime. His brief six months' spell of sickness had already broken me. If Pete had suffered for additional years, then decided to die, I'm not sure how we would have coped.

'But what am I meant to do now?' I said. 'Should I move house so I've no more memories of Pete? Or am I meant to stay here, close to where he's died?' I could feel tears welling up as the thought of Pete's demise started filtering through.

'Stop right there,' Henry said, shifting forward in his chair. 'I'd advise you to make no major decisions for at least a year.' I wasn't sure how I was going to do that. My mind was so muddled that, as far as I could see, I had two main decisions to make right there and then. The first was what I should have for dinner that night, because I was supposed to eat, and the second was whether I should move back to Africa and take up the work I used to do there. As far as my brain was concerned, these decisions were on a level par. 'Your sole priority is to look after yourself and your boys,' Henry said. 'That's all you should worry about right now.'

'But what do I tell them?' I knew that whatever was said, no matter how it was said, would leave a permanent scar. How do you explain to a three- and five-year-old the stark choice their father had just made?

'Whatever you do, don't lie to them,' Henry said, a warning in his tone. 'If you lie, they won't trust you later if you decide to tell them what really happened. Just be conservative with what truth you give them. Spoon feed them a little at a time.'

I nodded without thinking, trying hard to listen to Henry's cautionary words, to remember them all. All I could think was, if only Pete was here, he'd help me get through all this. He'd be the one giving me advice on how to handle this disaster.

Henry didn't try and predict my future, to forewarn me how hard things would be; neither did he try and convince me that everything would be okay. I appreciated his honesty. He left with some valuable parting advice. 'Say yes to everything,' he said. 'If someone asks you to go for coffee, say yes. If someone offers to mind the kids, say yes. You'll not want to bother people; at times you'll not feel like seeing people, but in my experience, saying yes will help you get through this time.'

It was getting dark, around 4 pm, when the police arrived back at my door. I hadn't even noticed that they had left, such were the comings and goings. I realise now that we were lucky that they had found Pete's body so quickly, the same day that he disappeared. With darkness falling, we could have been left wondering, waiting anxiously the whole night before the search could resume come morning. The police brought Pete's phone with them, which they had found in his possession. I needed to access it now, to note down numbers of friends who had to be informed. With his death, there was a funeral to organise. I assumed most would wish to come.

I made call after call, all in the same tone. 'I'm really sorry to be phoning like this, but Pete passed away today.' With Pete's friends having no prior warning of any illness, the silence on the other side was deafening. I filled the void with the detail they were looking for, 'He went for a run this morning and didn't come home. I'm sorry, but he took his own life.' There was nothing more I could say. Numbness on my part rendered the job bearable. It wasn't that I had come to terms with what had happened. My apparent calmness came from being in such a deep state of shock that I was operating on autopilot.

When I could make no more calls, I turned to social media. Pete had friends all over the world, having worked throughout the UK and Ireland, the United States, Asia and Africa. It was the quickest way to inform everyone that Pete was no longer with us. I picked out a photo of Pete to post online, at a time when he was happy. We had just returned to Ireland, back in 2012, full of hopes of settling and starting a family. I wondered what would have happened if I had told him right then that he only had six more years to live.

The messages of condolence came thick and fast on my screen. Disbelief resonated. They were so sorry for my loss. It was such terribly sad news. Their thoughts and prayers were with the boys and me at this difficult time. No one knew he had been ill.

With the children away, and Pete's brother and wife staying with me, I slipped away to my bedroom when the clock told me it was time to sleep. I lay there, acutely aware of Pete's absence on his side of the bed. There was a part of me still in deep denial; feeling like Pete was just away on another business trip, that he'd be back home once the assignment was complete.

Despite knowing that I should rest, my thoughts went into overdrive.

Tiredness evaded me. Instead my mind went round and round in circles, trying to make sense, replaying conversations, reliving moments, wondering what had just happened.

Eventually I had had enough. I got out of bed and slipped away to the living room to communicate with the outside world. So many around the planet were reaching out to me. Friends were devastated, in shock, so sorry to hear my news. They were thinking of me, praying for us, asking for strength on our behalf. I replied to them all, explaining that it had been depression, that he'd not slept in months, that it was suicide.

I was surprised when one person in particular reached out. I didn't know her that well. We had squared up against each other in many races, fought against each other for podium places, and cordially congratulated each other once we had both crossed various finish lines. I didn't know Fiona Meade that well outside of these race scenarios, and yet here she was messaging me at 5 am, trying so hard to find the right words.

'I'm so sorry,' she said in her message when I told her it was depression that had pushed Pete over the edge. 'It's terrible to think someone so loved can feel so desperately alone in life.' It was calming, yet surprising, to hear that she totally understood what I was going through.

I had known my mountain-running friend and fellow Wicklow Round completer, Eoin, for many years. I had run with him, biked with him, had pints with him, but never knew, until I bumped into him that day at the film screening that he lived in the shadow of his father's death. Now Fiona revealed to me why she could empathise so well; because her own brother Brian had taken his own life at the age of twenty-eight.

Little do we know what is really happening in people's private lives.

I reached out to Fiona. 'Tell me how to survive this,' I messaged.

'The only thing that helped me was thinking that finally his mind was at peace, that he could rest,' she wrote. 'He was no longer a tortured soul.'

Rest in Peace. RIP. I had seen these words for years, yet only now did they really make sense. Pete had been so tormented by his incessant thoughts, his sleepless nights, his anxiety and all-encompassing hopelessness, how could I not wish him to have some peace at last, to finally rest?

Fiona and I continued to message back and forth in those early hours, as I tried to make sense of what had just happened, while she revealed how the passing of years had helped her to come to terms.

'I know a lot of people say suicide is selfish, but I really disagree,' Fiona said. She explained how her brother had reached a point where he was convinced he was a waste of space, a burden on those he loved. His sense of self-worth had been completely decimated. She told me Brian ended up believing that the world would be better off without him. Only with time had Fiona understood Brian's rationale, borne from his mental illness. From his place of darkness, Brian decided he would make things easier for everyone.

I re-read Fiona's message again and again, wondering how she knew that that was how Pete had told me he felt. How did she know that one of the final conversations I had with Pete ended with him saying, 'I'm such a bad husband and father'? It was like depression had reprogrammed Pete's brain, making him say and do exactly what Fiona's brother Brian had said and done. Pete also truly believed we'd be better off without him, even though nothing could have been further from the truth.

Much later I found out why Fiona was even up at the ungodly hour of 5 am and able to reach out to me at that time. I didn't know it then, but she had recently given birth, and was awake to feed her hungry newborn son.

In remembrance of her brother, whose life had been cut short far too soon, she had named her child Brian.

In my silence, Fiona reached out with a prayer that had helped her, before signing off. 'God called your name so softly that only you could hear; no one heard the footsteps of angels drawing near. His golden gates stood open, God saw you needed rest. His garden must be beautiful, because he only takes the best.'

Dawn slowly leaked into the house with me barely registering its presence. Despite having no sleep, I felt wide awake. I knew I could no longer put off telling my children. I called my friend, who brought them back to me.

They were full of sleepover excitement when they bounded back into the house. They wanted to tell me about the ice-cream they ate, about watching Power Rangers on TV late into the night, how they slept in bunk-beds and fought over who got the top one.

'Come to me, my little ones. Can we sit down for a while?' I said, guiding them into the living room and towards the couch. I sat my eldest, Aran, on my knee, whilst Cahal continued to do somersaults on the rug. Hard as I tried, I couldn't make my three-year old sit still. My friend signalled that she'd be in the hall if I needed her, and softly closed the door.

I took a deep breath and began.

'Do you remember how Daddy was sick?' I asked them, a little relieved that they at least knew this part of the story. Pete didn't want them visiting him in hospital while he was there for treatment, but I had brought them on the hour-long round trip twice a week regardless.

'Was that when he was in hop-stipal?' Aran asked.

'Yes, you remember the doctors in hospital?' I said. 'Well, I'm so sorry

Aran, Cahal, but the doctors weren't able to make Daddy better.' I held Aran close, trying to protect him from what I would say next. 'Daddy died yesterday.'

With those words, Aran understood. His body curled up tight, so tight into a ball, as if defending himself from this onslaught of hurt.

'Daddy died?' he said, his voice small and sore. 'So is he in heaven?'

'Yes, of course he is, my dear,' I replied, trying to go along with whatever helped him process what I was telling him. I didn't need to explain how and why Daddy died. Just the fact that Pete was no longer with us was the nugget I would give them to process at this time.

'Cahal, Cahal,' Aran shouted. 'Daddy died and is in heaven.'

Cahal stopped his manic moves for a moment to come closer to us. 'Daddy's... Daddy's...' he managed, before letting out a gut-wrenching, soul-destroying cry. 'But who is going to give me horsey?' he wailed, before throwing himself on to the ground. If there was one thing Cahal loved, it was being hoisted on to Pete's sturdy shoulders and carried around at a height. He would squeal with delight, as Pete would clip-clop through the house with added horse-like sound effects. There would be no replacing that.

I went quickly to gather Cahal up off the floor, though it was I who needed gathering now. I called for my friend, who swiftly swung open the door and ran to my rescue. No one had warned me that this was the likely question a three-year-old would ask when they learned their Daddy was gone.

'Don't worry,' she said, as Aran and Cahal snapped back into their childhood and ran off to play with their toys. 'Cahal will be like this for a few months, but he's so young, he'll probably soon forget. Just keep an eye on Aran though, maybe get some help with counselling if you think he needs it.'

I looked on in bewilderment. I hadn't really figured out that it was not just my grief, but also that of my children, that I had to navigate as well.

If I was going to be able to process any of this, I had to get some sleep. Years of training for mountain races had taught me the importance of rest. My coach had made me keep a sleep diary, something he reviewed regularly, detailing how many hours I got and what the quality was like. Anytime I had slept less than eight hours, he had cautioned me. If medication was going to make me rest, then I knew I had to get some. I called the doctor's office and explained my situation. Within the hour, a prescription was produced to sedate me.

While I tried to do as Henry told me, to look after myself and my boys, Pete's brother and wife left to see the body at the mortuary. I had decided not to make the trip, John's advice still ringing in my ears. There was still plenty of time for me to see Pete later if I changed my mind.

They were both visibly shaken on their return.

'He looked well,' they said, as I made them some tea. I could see they were thinking carefully through their words. 'There's no…well, sign of how he died.' I didn't want to cut them off, yet couldn't bear the detail. I wasn't ready for an image of Pete's lifeless body to form in my mind. I nodded as I sat down opposite them. 'So we brought back…' they said, before handing me Pete's wedding ring.

And that was it. That was the moment when I knew Pete was really gone. I had given him that ring nine years before, committing to be with him in sickness and in health, until death did us part. The ring lay heavy in my hand, coming back to me full circle having fulfilled the promise we had made each other.

I could hold it in no longer. I broke down, sobbing uncontrollably. I could deny Pete's death no more.

CHAPTER 4

MOUNTAIN TRAINING

We will never truly know why Pete got sick. We can only guess the reasons why he wanted to die. But what I really want an answer to is, what happened to our plan?

I thought we had a plan.

Pete had always felt the pressure of being the main breadwinner in our family. It wasn't something I was entirely comfortable with either. We had made a joint decision though that, when the kids were born, I would stay home and care for them. At the time, it made sense for me to be a full-time mother.

As the babies became young boys, and as I emerged from a sleep-deprived post-natal haze, I soon found that I needed to do something more strenuous with my brain than just be a mum. 'You'll be bored when the kids go to school full-time,' Pete used to remind me as the children grew.

I agreed that I needed to do something with all the time I would eventually have on my hands once they both hit school-going age. So I enrolled to do a Masters in Environmental Engineering at Belfast's Queens University, starting in September 2018. I had always wanted to go back to developing countries, working there like I did in my twenties and thirties, but this time with the hope of focusing in the area of water and sanitation.

A couple of weeks before I was to begin, Pete became unwell. I quickly had to admit to myself that travelling up and down to Belfast for studies, as well as looking after a three- and five-year-old and a sick husband, would be too much. I asked the institution to delay my entry for another year.

This still left the issue of a household income. Pete had stopped taking on work, his brain unable to function at the high level it used to. I needed to find something that allowed me the flexibility to be there for my family while also giving me employment. Previously I had worked as an international-development consultant based from home. The only problem was that my former work often involved travelling to developing countries for a week, sometimes a fortnight, at a time. I couldn't leave my family for that long, not with the amount of care they all demanded.

Normally I would have talked through such difficult life choices with Pete. He was brilliant at helping me think through all the options, guiding me to make the best decision. Now, when I spoke to him about these dilemmas, he couldn't process what I was saying. He was stuck instead in the latest concern he had that day, unable to see out from its terrifying imagined consequences.

So I had to make an educated guess, on my own, at what was best for us. With the Mourne Mountains on my doorstep, and my background in mountain running, I decided I would set up a venture providing training and guiding in the sport. I could go part-time on the days of my choosing, so that I would be there for Pete and the boys, but still have a chance be in the mountains for work and respite.

The problem was, I wasn't too sure how to go about setting up such an enterprise. So I contacted other mountain runners I knew based in the UK who had similar companies. They all seemed to have outdoor qualifications, in particular something known as the Mountain Leader award. Although typically known as a hill-walking award, they assured me that this was the best way to get up to speed with navigation, group management, emergency first aid and a host of other skills that would be needed to bring people safely into the outdoors. It would cover all the bases, which I could then tailor for my mountain-running circumstances.

That is how I managed to find myself outside Northern Ireland's Tollymore National Outdoor Centre on a cold autumnal day, two months after missing my masters' enrolment date. I had signed up for their Mountain Leader award training course, which was to take place on three separate weekends over the coming months.

My eyes naturally gravitated to the Mourne Mountains that rose above the Centre. I had previously run over those granite peaks on many a mountain race, desperately trying to escape fellow competitors. I had now signed up to learn how to walk through them, to stop and think of others' well-being while out there, as opposed to doing whatever I could to shake off the people I was with. I wasn't sure if I was capable of such a radical slowing down or of demonstrating such levels of care and attention.

I entered the Centre to see three other trainees already waiting for our instructor. They were sitting around chatting and relaxing, indulging in some pre-course tea. From afar I could see that they were wearing gaiters and clunky hiking boots underneath the table, not the skinny inov-8 mudclaw shoes I was used to sporting. Their packs by their sides were sixty litres plus, with retractable hiking poles attached. I thought of my beloved four-litre bumbag that I'd left back home that carried nothing more than my mandatory kit, kit that I had pared down to the bare minimum to save on precious grams. To my fellow trainees, weight was not an issue. On the table they were packing up cheese and ham sandwiches and flasks full of hot tea for that day's mountain outing. I knew I'd look weird if I said I'd be fine with a gel and bit of water.

'Hi, I'm Caris,' one of the trainees said, extending her hand out towards me. 'Moire,' I said, returning her greeting before pulling a chair up to sit down.

'You're here for the...'

'Yeah, Mountain Leader training,' I said. I wasn't sure if I looked the part. I was very aware that my hiking boots were brand new, not having had the time to muddy them up before arriving. I had tried my best to blend in with hiking trousers and a thick fleece jumper, but deep down I knew I was a fraud. 'I'm not much of a walker...' I said.

'Oh, don't worry about that,' Caris quickly replied. 'Sure I'm a rock climber.'

'You'll have no problem then with the course's rope-work,' I said, slightly envious of her head start. I had been warned that part of the Mountain Leader award required knowing how to bring people down off mountains using emergency rope techniques. I was dubious that I'd ever need that skill. There was no way I was going to be running around the hills with a thirty-metre rope in my pack, just in case a fellow mountain runner had taken an ill-advised shortcut off a cliff. According to the racing rules, as I understood them, that would have been their prerogative.

'Yeah, but my navigation is really bad,' Caris replied. 'I'll have to get out and practise if I want to qualify.' With the mention of navigation, I suddenly felt at ease. Out of the entire syllabus, the use of a map and compass was my defining strength. I had competed in two-day moun-tain marathons, a race where you must navigate between random points strewn across mountains while being totally self-sufficient. I had entered the Irish Rogaine several times, an event where you need to find as many mountain checkpoints as you can within twenty-four hours using only a map and compass. I had finished the mountain-running endurance challenges, the Wicklow Round south of Dublin and the Denis Rankin Round in the Mournes. All these events demanded that mountain runners could self-navigate, and my successful completion of them made me confident that I already had the prerequisites.

Our instructor, Sean, soon arrived, and after an inspection of that day's weather forecast, we were bussed out towards the mountains. Within five short minutes, we hopped out at the start of Trassey's Track, one of the many gateways to the Mournes.

'So where are we on the map?' Sean asked us as soon as we had our rucksacks buckled up. Heads went down, maps were turned, compasses aligned with magnetic north. I wasn't sure what all the fuss was about, yet wondered if I was missing a trick. I had run down Trassey's Track so often that it was obvious which line we were standing on.

I pointed the track out on the map to Sean, who just let out a short sigh in return. Then Caris piped up, 'We're right on this slight track bend, because I can hear the river to our right.' Sean seemed infinitely more pleased with Caris's response. I had showed him where we were within a hundred meters, good enough to find a checkpoint in a mountain race. What I had failed to realize that he expected greater accuracy; that his version of 'where are we on the map' needed to be within five meters. Our instructor moved swiftly on from my mistake.

'So if we are to journey along the track to the sheep's pen on your map, how long will it take us?' Sean asked. Now I was totally thrown. For all I knew, the time it would take depended on the pace I was running, which depended on whether it was an ultra I was competing in or a short and sharp five-kilometre course. It would also depend on the terrain, whether the path was rutted or bouldered or flooded or muddy or grassy, something that the map we were using couldn't tell us. It would probably also depend on my resting heart rate that morning and no doubt involved my given glycogen levels. Somehow, I didn't think this was the answer that Sean was looking for.

Another trainee, Benji, came to our collective rescue. 'Well, the path is five hundred metres long with twenty metres of climb, so we should get there in nine and a half minutes.' My jaw nearly dropped. If I were doing interval sessions, I'd easily cover double that distance in half that time.

Sure enough, when we got to the sheep's pen, over nine minutes had passed. I didn't know if I was to be amazed by Benji's predictions, or depressed that half a kilometre from now on would take me so long.

Fortunately my bewilderment was quickly banished by the views. The majestic Mournes were now wonderfully close up, with the towering tors of Slieve Bearnagh peeking out from behind Spellack's slabs. I could see Caris salivating at the idea of heading up Spellack and its sleek rock faces, abandoning her navigation exercises for a spot of trad climbing.

'So does anyone know how Hare's Gap was formed?' Sean said, interrupting our general mountain gazing to focus our attention to a close-by feature. I knew that Hare's Gap was the impressive mountain pass that lay before us, a U-shaped chunk carved out from the terrain. It was the place where, on the annual Seven Seven's mountain race you'd run through while looking up at Slieve Bearnagh in front of you thinking, 'Oh God, do I have to climb that?' That's where my knowledge abruptly ended.

None of us trainees were sure of Hare's Gap's origins, something Sean was happy to put right. He revealed to us that it was formed thanks to glacial erosion around 14,000 years ago, with ice retreating on both sides of this granite rock. Geology was never my strong point at school, but I was starting to realise that it was yet another requirement of this multi-faceted qualification.

'Hare's Gap was also popular with smugglers in the eighteenth century,' Benji then volunteered. This, I knew, could be interesting. 'They used to land contraband goods like soap, leather, spices, and brandy at Bloody Bridge, then hike them across the mountains.' Sean seemed suitably impressed. All I knew about the Brandy Pad was that it was a really good route choice in the Mourne Mountain Marathon if you had checkpoints on both the western and eastern sides of the range. I had never really questioned why the path was there in the first place or why it was called the Brandy Pad. Had I been missing something after all these years of racing because of my incessant quest for the podium?

We journeyed on up Trassey's Track, timing each leg as we did. I saw the other trainees referring to laminated, tabulated cards that told them how long each leg would take for different distances at different speeds. I couldn't help wondering if that was cheating.

Soon we scaled a minor peak, which Sean wanted us to stand on for a while. 'Put yourselves on the contour,' he soon told us. I was a little con-fused. I knew we were in and around the summit, thereabouts, but how could you stand on a line that was only visible on the map, not physically on the ground? When it became obvious to him that we were all in the wrong place, he started to unleash his frustration. 'Do you not see how the ground twists and turns and moves in and out?' He walked us around the dips and over the curves, excited by the exotic shape of the terrain.

Slowly I started to see what he meant. I hadn't really stopped to have a good look at the landscape before, to really appreciate how the cartographer had so lovingly traced the ebbs and flows of the land. I was starting to feel slightly ashamed that I had spent so much time in the mountains but never really slowed down to appreciate their subtle shape and size.

All the hanging around also made me realize that the gear I was wearing was really meant for running, not for standing still. I had worn loads of layers in an attempt to blend in better, to look more like a hill walker. Despite my additions, I shivered beneath their fast-wicking fabrics, as the others seemed snug in their puffy down jackets and Polartec thermals. Even my expensive waterproof jacket was all wrong, too ultra-lightweight in comparison with the oversized, storm-proof, bomb-proof ones everyone else was wearing. I put clothing on my growing list of things I needed to rectify.

Thankfully, Sean got us moving again, this time to do an exercise in pacing. I had used this technique before, mainly when orienteering. It is based on the idea that your stride length remains predictable when travelling over a set distance. Typically orienteers know how many paces they do, the number of times the same foot hits the ground, when covering one hundred metres. Sean pointed to a nearby wall that marked the boundary between some fields and the mountain.

'I want you all to pace from this summit to that wall, and tell me the distance you get.' Everyone lined up and started marching towards it in silence. 'One…two…three…four…' we all muttered under our breaths, carefully counting our strides. I hit the brickwork, then did a quick mental calculation of how far I had just travelled. 'Two hundred and eighty metres,'

I declared when Sean asked me my figure.

'Two hundred metres,' the other trainees chimed back in unison. I was out by eighty metres. I could have been out by eighty miles as far as Sean was concerned.

What I hadn't taken into account was that my running stride, wearing sleek feather-light trail runners, is slightly longer than my walking one when my feet are clad in clunky hiking boots.

It was starting to dawn on me that I was not going to breeze through this Mountain Leader award as I had initially planned. I still had to learn about steep ground techniques, synoptic charts, flora and fauna, group management, risk assessments…the list seemed never-ending. Even the one thing I thought I was competent in, navigation, I was far too haphazard with.

Despite this realisation, I knew I had no choice but to continue with the training. It was the only way I could see that would give me the flexibility of working while continuing to be there for my dear Pete and our precious children.

CHAPTER 5

QUALITY DAYS

There was a four-week break before the next training weekend, a time we could use to get out into the mountains and practise some of the navigation techniques we'd learned. Not only did we need to perfect our map and compass skills if we wanted to pass the award, but we also needed to start logging something known as 'Quality Mountain Days' or QMDs. The Award's governing body, the Mountain Training Association, lists certain criteria that defines what a QMD is, things like a journey in the mountains of more than five hours, travelling off-trail, ascending a peak, all within a designated mountainous area within the UK and Ireland.

The easiest time for me to log QMDs was during the week, when the boys were at playgroup and school. One morning I was preparing to head out for such a session when Pete took a turn for the worse. He was becoming increasingly paranoid, afraid for his personal safety. I tried to calm him down in between getting the boys ready and myself prepped for the mountain. Nothing I said, however, would ease Pete's state of mind.

As I drove Aran and Cahal to their respective classes, I felt a growing sense of unease. I had never seen Pete as bad. So once I had dropped them off, I turned the car around and returned home to check on Pete. I found him pacing the floors, looking more anxious than ever.

'Let's go,' I said, taking his hand and dragging him towards his wardrobe. 'Get your thermals on. Bring a hat, some gloves, and put on your waterproof coat.' He looked at me bewildered. 'I can't leave you here like this,' I said. 'You're coming with me to the mountain.'

'But I don't want to ruin your...'

'Forget it,' I said, asserting my authority. 'I need to practise leading groups in the mountains anyhow. I'll pretend you're my client.' I'd have preferred to have gone on my own, to have had a break from everything, but I knew that wasn't possible.

Pete obediently put on some outdoor clothes while I went to the kitchen to pack some extra food.

'That footwear should be fine,' I said when he returned, pointing to his runners. Pete was not a mountain person and had even less hillwalking gear than me. Despite having lived beside the Mourne Mountains for over three years, he had barely ventured into them. The weather looked mild, however, so I knew that he could get away with the basic items he was wearing.

I tried to make small talk as we undertook the fifteen-minute drive towards Ott car park, where I intended to start from. 'So we'll just hike up to the col, and if we're feeling okay, we'll walk on over to Doan, then make our way back from there.' Pete barely registered what I was saying. He didn't even reply. I wasn't all that surprised. He was so deep in his thoughts and worries those days that he rarely engaged me in light conversation. The only things he could speak to me at length about were his growing, overwhelming anxieties that I had no remedy for.

I carried on chatting regardless, before parking the car, then crossing the road to the stile and the start of the main path. The outdoors are supposed to be good for people suffering from depression. Maybe if I taught Pete a couple of skills, got him interested in the mountains, he would spend more time in them and reap the apparent benefits. Perhaps this is what Pete needed to help him get better.

I resolved not to talk of what was worrying him that day, but to speak purely of the hills. I showed him our location on the map and the features that confirmed our whereabouts. I pointed out any interesting contours I could find, trying to ignite in him the excitement Sean had shown at the undulating landscape around us during our training weekend.

On reaching the impressive Mourne Wall after an hour's hike, I couldn't help but try to distract Pete with a bit of historical knowledge that I'd crammed in. 'Did you know this dry-stone wall is a total of thirty-two kilo-metres long, and took eighteen years to build, from 1904 to 1922?' I said, barely taking a breath. 'It passes over fifteen mountain summits and was put in place to protect the water catchment area around Silent Valley Res-ervoir.' I pointed in the direction of the peaks, tracing the line of the wall as it journeyed towards Slieve Donard, Northern Ireland's highest mountain. I watched Pete's gaze take in the serenity of the Mournes, hoping the view would somehow lift his mood and feelings.

'Ready to go?' I asked, trying to be a good group leader. Pete nodded, and not wanting to give him a chance to change his mind, I marched us towards Doan. The mountain was a particular favourite of mine. It's an odd cone shape in the midst of the range, with formidable steep cliffs around its summit. It's reached by bog-hopping a stretch, then travelling across a strange lunar-like landscape, before starting a short sharp climb to its top. I had particularly fond memories of the peak, it being part of the Lough-shannagh route that's on the summer Hill and Dale mountain-running series. The one time I had taken part in the race, I was stunned to see locals descend its steep terrain so swiftly, fleet footed like billy goats, heedlessly flinging themselves down Doan's near vertical slopes.

I could see Pete was lagging a little as we made our way out to Doan. He was still running quite regularly, but his energy levels were noticeably low, and our mountain jaunt was proving tiring. He hadn't spoken, however, of his latest woes. I wasn't sure if this was because the mountains had melted them away, or because he didn't want to bother me with them. Regardless it was nice to have a break from discussing them.

We sat down on Doan's summit where I produced some baked goodies to eat. 'It's lovely here,' I said, passing him a brownie. 'I'm always amazed how I can come out here and so often have the whole place to myself. It's beautiful, isn't it?'

Pete hesitated a beat before replying, 'Yes, it is.' I wasn't convinced by his answer.

'You know,' I said, unsure if I would regret bringing up his affliction. 'I recently read that depression is like having your feelings wiped out, like you look at something and you know it's beautiful but you don't feel any of that beauty.'

Pete turned to face me, sadness etched across his face. 'Yeah, that sounds about right.'

The idea of sitting in the mountains, with a fat chocolate brownie, together with your soul mate, in the fresh air and sunshine, and not feeling a thing. That thought made me want to cry as well.

Pete probably sat there on the summit for my benefit, but there was no need for us to hang around. I knew I had to get back to collect the children by 2 pm. As I got up to go, I showed Pete on the map where we had travelled, and how we would use a compass to guide us back home.

'So if you calculate a bearing like that,' he said. 'How do you know which way to go?'

'You just need to follow the direction of travel arrow,' I replied, pointing it out on the baseplate, 'while keeping the needle boxed.'

Handing over my compass, I let him take the lead. I watched him steadying it before looking far into the distance to pick a spot. He then moved carefully over the broken boggy ground in the direction we needed to go.

'That's perfect,' I said. 'Nice job.' I started to rattle on about when you'd need to use the compass in misty conditions, and how you'd probably use a slightly different route with handrails and attack points. Part of me was just practising the spiel I planned to use if I was teaching a mountain runner how to navigate. The other was just desperately trying to distract Pete, to keep him focused in the here and now, to keep his mind purely in the mountains.

Sadly, it was not to last. Though I had seen glimpses of the old Pete while he was busy navigating, as soon as we returned to the car park, his dark cloud was already there, patiently waiting for him. I had managed to give him only a momentary reprieve with our outing. It was a sad lesson to learn; that despite so many extoling the virtues of the outdoors and exercise to treat depression, it doesn't work for everyone. Pete had given up alcohol and caffeine, was meditating, was attending counselling, was taking medication, was reading books, was exercising, was doing social activities with the kids, yet none of these apparent remedies for depression seemed to work.

After our mountain walk, over the following weeks, things went from bad to worse. Pete's sister arranged for him to go stay with her for a couple of days, to give the boys and I a short break. Because I was living with Pete day in, day out, I hadn't noticed how ill he had become. It had been a slow and steady decline. His sister, not having seen him properly for months, was astounded by how bad Pete was now that his illness was entrenched.

During his short time with her, Pete admitted that he had been researching on the Internet how to commit suicide. Everyone went berserk. Normally Pete told me everything, absolutely everything that was going on in his life. This piece of crucial information he had somehow failed to mention.

'If he's looking this up, I'm not sure I can keep him safe,' I said, once we had brought him back home and got him straight in to see his counsellor. His counsellor and I sat together in a small clinical room, with Pete sitting shrunken in the corner on a plastic-coated chair.

'But it wasn't like I was going to do anything,' Pete said. 'I was just…I just wanted to know…' His counsellor and I sat there, trying to give him space. 'Look it, I don't even know why I did it. I'm sorry.' I really did believe him. His counsellor, however, was not so sure, and Pete's family even less so.

Though it was the last thing I wanted, his counsellor asked Pete to agree to be admitted to a mental health unit in a local hospital. Pete looked up at me as she spoke. He resembled a lost three-year old, begging his mother not to abandon him. My heart bled. I didn't know what to do anymore. The only thing I knew for sure was that I was not qualified to help him. Maybe a spell on a ward would help. Maybe it would provide him with a different therapy. I thought it was at least worth a try.

And so it was that, just a week before my second mountain-leader training weekend, Pete was admitted to hospital. My head was in a tailspin. I needed to be there for Pete, though I recognised that he was in better hands now than when he was at home with me. I made the hour-long journey to the hospital for the sixty-minute visiting spots, sometimes bringing the children as a welcome distraction. I brought Twister, library books, Snakes and Ladders, so we could do family time as opposed to talk about depression.

When I went on my own, Pete would beg me to bring him home with me on my return. 'Just give it a few more days,' I would say in reply, feeling so guilty for having encouraged him to self-admit in the first place. When he saw I would not relent, we would sit there, side by side on the wipe-clean couch, in silence. I would take his hand and hold it close. He would slowly rest his head against my shoulder. He told me he wanted to cry, but didn't know how to. I had never seen him so broken.

Pete's brother agreed to visit Pete if I wanted to still attend the second training weekend. It meant that Pete would have company. I also desperately wanted to continue with the training, knowing the next available course wouldn't be held for months.

It wasn't until I arrived back at Tollymore Outdoor Centre that I realised the toll that Pete's sickness had taken on me. The second weekend involved security on steep ground and emergency rope work, two areas that I was very nervous on. We were driven to Carrick Little, on the southern part of the Mourne Mountains, allowing us access to the crags around Lower Cove. As soon as we started to hike towards the rocky outcrops, my defences suddenly failed me.

'So how have you been keeping?' Caris asked me as we walked along the track. It was such an innocent question, not intent on upsetting me. If I had been indoors, within the safe confines of an office or house, I think I could have pulled off a suitably nonchalant reply. But there is something about being outdoors, about doing some exercise, that always makes me talk about things that are on my mind.

'My husband is in hospital,' I said, feeling the pressure of the past few weeks suddenly rise with me. 'He's...he's not been well.'

'I'm so sorry to hear that,' Caris replied, such kindness in her voice. I barely knew Caris, and yet there was something about walking side-by-side that let me open up.

'Yeah, he's been suffering from depression,' I said, spilling the beans. 'Hopefully he'll get better soon.' Just saying those simple words, admitting to his socially unacceptable disease, before setting them loose within the mountains' expanse made me feel slightly better. It was cathartic, just like the tears that were now streaming down my face, tears that I let flow freely. If Caris had asked, I would have said it was the wind that was making my eyes water. But she didn't notice, and if she did, she made no remark. Without planning it, our stroll into the heart of the mountains was deeply cathartic.

Once we arrived at the steep rutted ground, I snapped straight into mountain-leader mode. Our task was to guide our fellow trainees up and down scree gullies, deciding where to position ourselves to make sure we broke any potential slip, stumble or fall. We peered over cliffs, making critical judgements whether we would dare to bring groups down them. We practised using reassuring yet guiding words to each other, pretending we were in an emergency situation and needing to maintain absolute calm. It was so high intensity that I didn't have time to think about Pete or his illness or his treatment or the effect this was having on our family and future. It was the distraction I needed, a chance to let my mind think of something, anything else.

It was like I had two separate life-threatening challenges going on simultaneously. At least with my mountain-leader training, I felt I had some element of control.

The next day we journeyed to the cliffs around Pigeon Rock to learn emergency rope techniques. I struggled to comprehend what knots to make and where to place them even though I was told a granny knot at the end of the rope would nearly always suffice. My brain couldn't coordinate the process of belaying, the slipping and sliding and pulling of the rope that would keep a person on the other end safe. I made bad decisions around suitable anchors, opting to tie my rope around boulders that slid down the mountainside with the slightest knock. I wasn't sure if it was because I was getting older and struggling to learn new skills. Or was it because I was under such pressure at home that I was incapable of processing anything new?

I left the training weekend shell-shocked by what was required of me. My only consolation was that rock-climber Caris also struggled. She admitted that the techniques required were so simplified from what she was used to that it was like learning them all anew. It seemed like I needed to plan some QMDs that involved perfecting my rope work.

Two weeks after Pete was admitted, we all agreed that he was well enough to leave the unit. Christmas was just around the corner, and we all wanted Pete to spend time at home with our family. He also hated the ward with a passion. 'I'm not like these other patients,' he told me every time I visited. 'They're all crazy.' I couldn't help agreeing with him that he wasn't suffering in the same way as them. Pete really wasn't that bad.

We made the most of the time in the run up to Christmas, going on daily outings with the boys. Pete seemed better, a little better, something I assumed was thanks to his change in medication. The consultant had cautioned me that it could take four to six weeks to see its full effects, but already I thought Pete was improving.

Christmas Day, Pete struggled out of bed, nothing unusual there. As the day progressed, however, his mood slowly lifted. He even phoned friends and family after dinner, people whose calls he had shunned for months, to wish them a happy Christmas. And when we finally pulled out Junior Monopoly that evening I finally saw my old Pete. He was back to his former self, buying up properties heedlessly, being far too competitive at this children's version of the game in an all-out effort to win. He rattled his dice raucously, laughing heartily as he handed over pretend money to his sons. Pete, my dearest Pete, had finally come back home.

They say that those who have decided to take their own life, those who have a specific plan put in place, can experience a sense of calm before they commit the final deed.

He was doing so much better that I thought it was safe to go to the Turkey Trot mountain race the next day, Boxing Day. I also wanted to spend some time with fellow mountain runners and to be in the Mournes for a while. It meant that night I was tired, too tired to do normal bath, book and bed duties for the boys.

'Is it okay if I lie down early?' I asked Pete. 'Maybe you get the boys to bed?' Pete agreed without question. As I lay there in the darkened room, I wondered if he regretted taking me up on my suggestion. I heard both boys screaming as someone else performed the nightly routine I normally delivered. They didn't want washed, they didn't want changed, they didn't like the books he suggested. I considered getting up, to relieve Pete from their stress, but didn't have the energy. What I did hear instead was Pete being amazingly patient. If he had been well, he would have got frustrated, would have asked me to take over, probably would have shouted at the boys for not obeying him. Instead I heard him quietly consoling them, cajoling them into their beds.

I snuck out to see him kissing them both gently on their foreheads. 'I love you, Aran. I love you, Cahal,' he said. It is only now that I realise that that was his final farewell.

I know that Pete loved his children dearly, more than anything in the world. I believe deep down that Pete desperately didn't want to die. It was just that he was suffering so much that he could no longer bear the thought of living. Depression had convinced Pete that Aran and Cahal would have an infinitely better life without him. If Pete had been uncaring, insensitive, unkind, he wouldn't have cared about what happened to his offspring or what his depression was doing to his family or friends. But because he loved us all so much, just like Fiona's brother Brian loved his family, he believed it was best for everyone if he made the ultimate sacrifice. Pete was convinced it was best he died so that we could keep on living.

CHAPTER 6

PETE'S WAKE

Pete and I had both agreed that, when we died, we wanted to be cremated. We had shared this over a relaxed dinner before getting married, during one of those romantic evenings where the conversation strayed comfortably between random themes.

'I'd like my ashes spread in the Wicklow Mountains,' I had said. I had spent so much time in their midst, preparing for the Wicklow Round and other races, that I thought it would be apt I went back there once I was done running round this earth.

'And I'd like mine spread in the mountains too,' Pete replied, 'the Comeragh Mountains.'

'You're just copying me,' I retorted. 'You don't even go into the mountains, unless I make you. At least my choice makes sense.'

Pete was visibly upset. What I had failed to recall was that Pete had grown up on a rural farm in County Waterford. From his childhood bedroom window, the Comeraghs towered before them, a rugged mountain range punctuated by deep glacial lakes. On trips we'd make to visit his family, the Comeraghs were always the first thing we'd see as we drew close to his homestead, a sure sign to Pete that we were nearly there. Once I understood his rationale, I relented and let him share my post-funeral cremation plan.

So when the undertaker asked for clothes to dress Pete in, I knew that whatever I chose was going to go up in flames. Pete looked his best in work clothes, always immaculately presented in his CEO suit and tie. I knew that that was what we had to dress him in. I went to Pete's wardrobe, bracing myself, before edging open its door. Turning the light on, I saw all his shirts, trousers and jackets lined up perfectly in a row on the rail, flawlessly ironed and hung. It was up to me to decide which combination would be the last one Pete would wear.

Pete was the head ironer in our household. There was nothing he found more relaxing than getting the ironing board out on a Sunday afternoon, holding a large bottle of spray starch in one hand and a remote control in the other. He'd watch rugby highlights on TV while meticulously removing wrinkles from his shirts, forcing razor-sharp creases into their sleeves. His domesticity was a welcome hangover from his days working at the US accounting firm, Arthur Anderson, where they had taught their recruits that presentation was key. Having never myself worked in the commercial world, Pete didn't trust me to do a good enough job, so I gladly left him to it.

Seeing his suits hanging there, gathering dust, suddenly made me feel so sad. It was all such a waste, a terrible waste, Pete dying so young at forty-nine. Pete had still so much life in him, so much more to give.

I flicked through them slowly, scraping their hangers along the railing, trying to find the one I could offer up in smoke. I soon found an immaculately pressed jacket that I hated, but one Pete used to love to wear. He had found it in a high-end charity shop and had bought it for a fiver. He was so proud of his find that day, declaring it a true bargain, even though it was decidedly ill fitting and had the world's scratchiest material and ugliest buttons. Despite my hatred of it, I found myself unable to part with it just because of that stupid memory.

Eventually I found a suit and shirt that I didn't remember Pete wearing, one that had no emotionally charged tales attached. I put it together with a red tie I found. Pete would often put on that tie in the morning, then ask my honest opinion. I always told him I preferred the purple one. At least now I was letting him wear this red tie he liked but I thought never suited him.

Once I knew what Pete would wear, I had to choose a coffin. Less than forty-eight hours after Pete's disappearance, it was all becoming very real.

When we'd dine out, I'd always let Pete make the wine selection. Though he pretended to be a true connoisseur, I was aware he knew very little. It didn't take long before I figured out his wine selection technique. His trick was not to choose the cheapest bottle on the menu, because there was probably a good reason for its rock-bottom price. Instead, Pete always chose the second cheapest wine off the menu. In keeping with this strategy, I requested Pete to be placed in the undertaker's second cheapest coffin. I knew Pete would have approved of my choice.

As the final details came together, it became apparent that the best place to have Pete's wake and funeral was back in Waterford, in the village where he was born and raised. I drafted a post to place on social media for those who wished to attend. Together with the time and place, I issued a simple request. Instead of flowers or donations, I asked people to bring along letters addressed to Pete's sons. I wanted them to write to the boys, to tell them who their father really was. With them being still so young, I was afraid that they would soon start to forget him. If Pete's friends and family wrote down their stories about Pete, I hoped that the boys, even if they didn't remember their father, would at least know who he was.

Once the funeral arrangements were in place, I travelled down to Waterford with my boys. Time in terms of days and dates no longer made sense. Instead I clung to the series of events that had to take place: wake, funeral, cremation in that order. And then? God only knew what happened once the formal rituals were done. My mind was physically unable to think that far ahead.

Once I arrived in Pete's home-place, I began to see the aftermath, of how far the shock waves of Pete's death had spread. I saw his father, his mother, his sisters, his aunts and uncles, his nieces and nephews, so stunned, so confused, so sad. Their grief compounded mine, with nothing to distract any of us from the fact of Pete's departure. It was all we could talk about. I seemed to repeat myself over and over, as well as hear the same words in return. 'I'm sorry for your loss'.

Eventually I needed out; I needed a break from it all.

'Is it okay if I go for a run? Could someone mind the boys for me for an hour?' The boys were busy playing with their cousins, happily catching up. There were so many adults milling around the house, I knew that the kids had ample babysitters.

Whenever Pete and I visited his home, 'the block' was our standard run. Just like back in Rostrevor, Pete rarely deviated from this circuit. Coming out of the farmstead, the route turned right, then followed a maze of quiet rural roads out towards the base of the Comeraghs before turning back. It was a simple ten kilometres that would at least get me out of the house.

I hadn't run since the Turkey Trot mountain race, since the day before Pete's death. My legs were hesitant, slow to get moving again, especially after the trauma of the preceding days. I knew it would do me good, however, to do a bit of exercise. Just like with my use of medication to sleep, I knew I had to do whatever it took to mind myself so that I could cope with the coming days.

As my body relaxed into the run, my mind soon loosened up. Only that, rather than playing tranquil thoughts, out came a barrage of unruly theories and questions. It replayed events from that day when Pete went missing. It retraced the months of his illness. It even delved back into our own decade of history, of the many choices and decisions we'd made together as a couple. I tried to distract it from this hurtling train of thoughts that were going to get me nowhere. Not even looking up at the mountains to find some positive inspiration could stop their negative trajectory.

I slowed to a gentle jog, trying to calm everything down. But then one thought came, detonating in my brain.

'You're a single mother now.'

I've no idea how I had avoided that obvious consequence of Pete's passing up until then. I tried to breathe, but the sudden realisation of being a single parent grabbed my throat, attempting to throttle me to death. I started to hyperventilate as the panic attack tightened its grip.

The only thing I could do was stop dead in my tracks. I bent over double in the middle of the road, hoping no traffic would come and bowl me over, fighting desperately to draw air in. I was slowly coming to terms with being called a widow, but now the 'single mother' label, and all its associated negative connotations, had thrust itself upon me.

It suddenly hit me that I would never be a part of a normal nuclear family, living with two children and their biological father, with a white picket fence and a dog. Instead I was thrust into a situation that I had not asked to be placed in, tagged with a title that I never imagined would be applicable to me.

Not even the knowledge that my single-mother friends had survived, were getting on with life, could assure me that all would be well.

After what seemed like a lifetime of wheezing in the middle of the road, I somehow managed to draw breath. I forced myself to take some slow steps. Fortunately my brain was starting to understand that, if a traumatic incident happens, it needed quickly squirrelling away. Just as fast as it had arrived, my sole-parenting fear was forcibly frog-marched to the back of my head. As soon as I could, I started to run once more, only this time more carefully in case another random assault was lying in wait.

There was another reason why I had to run home rather than slow to a walk. Before leaving the house, I was reminded that Pete was being trans-ported home that morning. His hearse was meant to arrive within the hour. I hadn't seen his body or his coffin up until then, and I didn't want to simply 'bump' into them on the road. The last two kilometres of my loop followed the same route that the hearse would have to take.

I sped up to get myself home as quickly as possible, before realising the strange irony. When he was alive, Pete always tried to beat me if we went for a run together. Even if I would protest that I was training, that I had to stick to certain heart zones or paces, he couldn't stop his competitive streak from coming out. If we participated in the same race, he'd be very quick to compare our splits and final times. There was a part of me that just couldn't let him, even in death, beat me to the finish line.

I kept looking over my shoulder as I ran, waiting to see the long black car swoosh past me on the final hill. Fortunately, I managed to reach the gate and run inside the house before the hearse arrived. I had beaten him home by mere minutes.

I realised I was still not ready to see Pete or even his coffin. John's words were still ringing in my ears, that I would never un-see Pete. So I decided to leave his family to prepare him for his wake, while I stayed close to my children.

I had brought with me one of Pete's business cards, a card from a company that he used to work for and where he had noticeably thrived. I passed this over to his family to be placed in his top pocket. I then realised that it would be apt if something from his children was placed with him as well. So I asked Aran to do a drawing for Daddy, to bring to heaven with him.

'Who's that?' I said to Aran when he had finally finished his picture.

'That's Daddy,' he said. 'And that's a road,' he continued, pointing to a black strip at Pete's feet. 'That's what he'll follow so he can come back home to us.'

There was no point arguing or explaining. I just wrapped my arm around his shoulder. With both of us looking on at his simple drawing I said, 'It's beautiful. I'm sure Daddy would love it.'

Things were getting more complicated by the minute. Now I had to refer to Pete in strange convoluted tenses. No longer could I say, 'Daddy will love it' or 'Daddy loves it,' the present and future tenses when talking of Pete now extinguished from our lives. I was struggling on so many levels.

I also hadn't explained to Aran and Cahal that their father was at that moment lying within the house. As far as they knew, Daddy was in heaven. I didn't know how I was meant to explain what a coffin was if their Daddy had already gone. If I wanted Aran's picture to accompany Pete on his final journey, it meant that I had to hide it away, have it placed in the coffin by someone else and hope that Aran wouldn't search for it later on. If Aran did ask for it, I had already concocted a story that the angels had brought the picture directly to Daddy. I hoped that one little white lie in the larger scheme of things wouldn't matter.

In rural Ireland, friends and family usually gather around their loved one back at their home rather than at a funeral parlour. The coffin is left open to allow them to see the deceased, for them to say their final goodbyes. It is also a social occasion that allows people to share their condolences with those who were closest to the deceased.

Wakes normally take place over a day or two. Unfortunately, due to the timing of his death, Pete's wake could only take place over a single evening for a couple of hours. The crematorium was closed on New Year's Day, so his funeral mass had to take place on New Year's Eve, with his wake on the preceding day. It gave everyone a very small window to visit Pete for the last time in the home he grew up in.

Keeping with my wish not to see Pete, I was placed in a small sitting room away from the main parlour where Pete lay. I glanced out of one of the room's windows, into the surrounding December darkness. Though I knew the main front door was around the other side of the house, all I could see outside were people lined up on the laneway, slowly shuffling forward, queuing to pay their respects. They were wrapped up in thick coats and warm hats, hiding their faces behind long scarves, patiently waiting their turn. None of this made sense. How could Pete have felt so alone when so many people obviously loved him, loved him so much to turn up for him on this cold and dark December night?

If anyone said to the ushers at the door they knew me, once they had said their farewells, they were directed towards the room I was in. So many people came towards me, people I hadn't seen in years. I knew many of them had travelled from the other end of the country at short notice just to pay their respects. Most of them said the same thing.

'We didn't know.'

'If we had known, we could have helped.'

'Why didn't he ask for help?'

Remorse and guilt were etched across their faces, as if they were somehow responsible by omission. I rushed to correct them as best I could. Pete's death was not their fault.

'He was depressed,' I explained. 'He didn't want anyone to know. He was tormented by the end.'

The problem was that Pete had gone so fast. Anyone who had seen him earlier in the year would have seen him in his normal flying form. I was one of the few who could shed a light on how sick he had become. In a way, I had lost him already six months beforehand. The shock of his death had been lessened for me knowing how much he had suffered; how much Pete wanted out.

And then one person in particular entered the room I was in. I knew Donal from the mountain-running scene. We were often at the same races that took place around Ireland and, though I didn't know Donal that well, we'd always exchange pleasantries if we bumped into each other at the start or finish line.

Donal was in floods of tears. I just couldn't understand it. Pete often accompanied me to these races, and would chat to anyone I'd talk to, just shooting the breeze. If Pete and Donal bumped into each other, they'd say hello, say a few things about the race or the weather, and then they'd be on their way. It wasn't like Donal really knew Pete, not like some of the others who I felt were justified in their tears.

'I'm so sorry for your loss,' he said, gasping for words between sobs. I didn't know what else to do except give him a big hug and thank him for travelling all the way. 'It's just that,' he said, breaking away from me to messily wipe his tears. 'My best friend also died this way.'

Just like Fiona, whose brother died from suicide, here was someone else I had known for many years, yet apparently never really knew at all. Here was someone else whose life had been irrevocably damaged by mental health issues, who lived with something that hurt so much that it was never deemed appropriate to bring it up in every-day conversation. Here was Donal who had lost a loved one because a disease made his friend believe that they were unworthy of his love.

I looked around the room all of a sudden with renewed eyes. So many of the shocked and saddened faces were of course because they had lost Pete without warning, their dear family member, beloved friend and respected colleague. But some of those desolate faces, I was slowly realising, were also carrying the weight of other deaths. Pete's death had served to reignite the memory of their own losses, forcing them to confront the grief they had hidden away yet still so obviously carried.

I continued throughout the evening to talk to mourners, to relay to them as best I could about Pete's illness and death, to explain exactly what had happened. I thought they had a right to know. I believed it would help them grieve.

As the evening wore on, I found that, the more I spoke about Pete's tragic fate, the less power the preceding events had over me. Every time I talked, I choked up a little less. Being open about mental health and suicide proved freeing.

For Pete, unfortunately, this revelation, that it was okay to talk about his mental health struggles, came too late.

CHAPTER 7

PETE'S FUNERAL

I woke up the next morning, dizzy from the concoction of sleeping pills I had taken to knock me out. Despite being exhausted from the wake, I still needed medication to make me rest.

I remember putting on dark clothes, layer upon layer of blackness, trying to make sure I looked right, that I did the right thing, whatever that was. No one had set me down and told me how I was meant to look, how I was meant to act on the day my husband was to be cremated.

I had already decided that the children would not go to the church or crematorium. I knew they were too young to sit still for the ceremonies. There was no point in trying to explain to them the rituals that were taking place. In addition, I was faced with another dilemma. Cahal was visibly unwell.

Three days before Pete died, Cahal had been potty-trained. It was like, just when Cahal had graduated out of nappies, Pete's disease convinced him that Cahal no longer needed him as a father. The only problem was that Cahal had not managed to do a number two since that day. I didn't know if it was the change in diet, the change in scenery, or the tangible stress that surrounded him. All I knew was that he was curled up in a ball on the sofa, holding his tummy, in considerable pain. We were all so busy with the funeral arrangements that no one had thought to get him treated. I had hoped it would self-resolve but, just as I was about to leave for the church, I realised that that was not going to happen. It was the first thing I was going to have to sort out once Pete's funeral was over.

Coming to terms with the fact that I would have to sit beside Pete's coffin throughout the ceremony, I knew I could no longer put off seeing it. Better I saw it within the privacy of the family home as opposed to in front of the congregation. With the hearse pulled up, ready to transport Pete to the church, I stood outside and steadied myself. Eventually, his closed coffin emerged from the house. People who loved Pete carried him aloft, visibly struggling under the load. Pete was a big man, a six-foot giant, a natural full back on the rugby field. Watching his friends and family carrying him so carefully, so lovingly, broke my heart. Pete would never have wanted to cause such pain. He would have been mortified that he had to rely on them to carry his remains.

Staring at the coffin, I tried to process what this all meant. I was still in deep shock, however, unable to understand the reality. My mind was still so fudged that random, unexpected thoughts kept filtering through instead. So when I saw the coffin being pushed into the car, all I could think was, 'Thank goodness Pete is now asleep.' Finally Pete was lying still, not tossing and turning in bed, or pacing the floors with terrifying thoughts. He was finally at peace, in a deep, deep sleep.

We drove the short distance to the church behind the hearse. Cars lined the narrow country road as we approached, a sign of just how many people had come to pay their respects. I had not anticipated, however, the sheer scale of the mourning crowd.

As I got out of our car, I stood waiting for Pete's coffin to be shouldered by more friends and relatives. People were spilling out of the church, with no room inside for them. I looked up and caught sight of two people I had not seen for over ten years, people whose company I dearly loved, but with whom I had lost contact. I couldn't help but smile at them. I was so grateful to see them. But then I remembered I was in mourning, that a smile was not appropriate. Instead, I started to feel guilty that it had to take the death of my husband for me to reconnect with them.

Things got worse as I entered the church itself. To my left and right, the pews were crammed full of Pete's favourite people. I saw friends young and old, from all stages of Pete's personal and work life. All I could think was, if Pete was here now, he would have been so, so, so happy. He would have let out one of his life-affirming roars, gone round and hugged and back-smacked every one of them. He would have ordered drinks for them from the local pub, and made sure to catch up on all their news over several pints. I would have had to drag him out of there at one o'clock in the morning so that the priest could lock up the place for the night. Pete would have been ecstatic with joy.

That happy thought of all Pete's favourite people in one place soon flipped to one of profound sadness.

'I thought we'd have more time,' I had heard people say over and over at the previous night's wake. 'I thought Pete and I would catch up later.' Why did we all leave it too late? Why did we never think to throw a big party and invite all of Pete's friends when he was still alive? Why did the amazing gathering happen only once he had died?

As I took my seat on the hard wooden bench designated for the family, I willed myself to be strong. I stared hard at his coffin that was in front of the altar, glad that the lid was now shut tight. I didn't need to see Pete's body to know he was gone, the sadness of his life sucked away. There was a portrait photo of him perched on top of the box, one I had taken on the Cliffs of Moher while Pete was walking Tom, our dog. He looked relaxed and happy. That's how I needed to remember him.

Together with this picture, there were symbols that represented Pete. A rugby ball, a Munster top and an All-Blacks scarf represented his love for the sport. A microfinance board-meeting folder showed his passion for his work. And a six-pack of Heineken bottles, a drink that he had shared with many of those present.

And so we prayed for Pete. We prayed that he would have a chance to read all the heartfelt messages that had been posted online about him since his passing. That he would know now that he was 'a smart, engaging man who genuinely cared about people', that he always made people laugh, that 'he was brilliant, charming, sweet and so interesting to talk to.' We prayed that he would finally know and truly believe that he was profoundly loved.

We prayed for Pete's children who had lost such an amazing father, and for all children who had lost parents. We asked that they be surrounded with love, that they would grow in wisdom and strength, and that we would be there as their extended family to comfort them in their need.

We prayed for Pete's family and friends who were mourning the loss of this caring, sensitive and witty man. We asked that they would find comfort in the forty-nine years' of memories that Pete had left us, and that we would continue to keep his memory alive.

We prayed too for all those who were suffering from poor mental health. We prayed for the wider community who care for them, that we would be compassionate and understanding enough to reach out to them in their need. And we asked that those who were suffering be reminded that it's absolutely ok not to be ok.

Finally, we prayed for the Irish Rugby team. That with Pete's heavenly help, they would continue their winning streak, lift the 2019 Rugby World Cup and become number one in the world.

Despite the personal touches that were littered throughout the ceremony, I was glad of the set piece of the Catholic mass that remained steadfast and unchanging. I knew where we were in the liturgy, how long I had left before I had to get up from my pew and accompany Pete on the final part of his journey.

What I didn't anticipate was the queue of people who wanted to share their condolences with me after the final blessing. I thought that everyone who wanted to say a kind word had already done so at the wake. I didn't know that many of those at the mass didn't go to that gathering, and so this was their opportunity to share a moment with me.

I stood up and faced the throng. A blur of faces shuffled past me, one after the other shaking my hand and whispering muffled awkward sentiments. One elderly lady, a family neighbour, I remember in particular. She took hold of my hand, and all I can recall was thinking how cold, how terribly cold her palm was. It was at that moment that I knew that I had made the right decision not to see Pete's body. Pete used to be the giver of the best hugs; warm all-encompassing cuddles that made me feel so safe and loved. If I went to hold Pete and not had my embrace returned, I don't know how I would have coped. If I had only felt coldness in exchange for my warmth, my heart would have irrevocably broken.

Then there was another lady, someone I did not know. She too wanted to share with me a few words, only her words were full of her own heavy grief that ended up spilling into mine.

'It's so hard,' she said, sobbing between her words. 'It's so incredibly hard.' I nodded gently, unsure of what to say or do. Later I was told she had also lost a loved one to a similar death. Seeing her, I started wondering if I was also going to become that type of person who would be hurled onto an emotional rollercoaster every time someone died, even if I didn't know them. Was I going to have any choice in how I'd react to Pete's death? Was I destined to live in despair for the rest of my days, to find life so arduous that I'd be unable to carry my grief?

More and more people filtered through: an old boss of mine approached, someone I didn't realise would care; someone who had been at the Turkey Trot race the day before Pete's death, someone I had briefly mentioned to while we ran shoulder-to-shoulder that Pete was not doing well; old school friends who had journeyed for half a day to be with me; people who had supported me on my Wicklow Round attempt a decade before, but who I had not seen since.

And then there were the many people who Pete had worked with. So many employees who Pete had mentored, coached and sorted problems out for; so many distinguished CEOs and board members who respected Pete. They said their names before telling me the organisation they worked for. I recognised a lot of their names from the times Pete would come home and tell me the crazy thing that had happened at the office that day. 'You'd never believe what so-and-so did...' would begin many a conversation.

Then an elderly man approached me, someone I didn't know.

'Frank Cummins,' he said. 'I'm sorry for your loss.'

I held on to his hand for a second longer than the others, a cog slowly turning in recognition. Then the penny dropped.

'Oh my God,' I thought, trying so hard to hide my gut reaction. 'It's

'Fuckin' Frank Cummins'.'

Pete had never called Frank by his proper name. He only had referred to him ever as 'Fuckin' Frank Cummins' due to the outrageous workplace politics the man always seemed to play.

'Pete,' I said inside my head, hoping that Pete would somehow hear. 'You're not going to believe it, but 'Fuckin' Frank Cummins' has come to your funeral.'

If Pete had been beside me right there and then, the fit and healthy version, I know he would have found this the funniest thing ever. This would have been the crazy story we would have shared for years to come, the idea that Fuckin' Frank Cummins was sad to see Pete gone. But Pete wasn't there to share this with. Pete was gone.

It was only the start of a long list of thoughts that would make me think, 'I'll share that with Pete when I see him next,' only for my brain to immediately stamp the idea out with the words, 'No, you won't, because Pete died.' I had no one to share these inside jokes and stories with anymore, no one who would find them interesting or funny like Pete always did.

Once the crowd subsided, it was time for Pete to be brought to the crematorium, an hour's drive away in Cork. While the pallbearers carried Pete one last time, I immediately spied the six-pack of Heineken bottles that lay un-opened near the altar. I grabbed them, hugging them close as I followed Pete's coffin. I knew I'd make good use of them later.

The crematorium itself was beautiful. Constructed on an island in Cork's harbour, it is a former magazine building built in the nineteenth century, used for housing gunpowder. Its arches now held stunning stained-glass windows, showering blue and white scenes of tranquillity around. All I could think was, Pete would love this place. It made me feel at peace, that

I had made the right decision, allowing him to share my post-funeral plan over that romantic, intimate meal.

A short ceremony was had, before an ornate slide drew closed across Pete's coffin. Just like that, he was physically gone. I was informed that Pete's ashes would be available within the week. Deep down, I knew that it would be at their spreading that I would really have a chance to bid farewell. Despite my Catholic upbringing, the farmhouse wake, the church funeral, the dignified crematorium, none of these ceremonies had struck a chord with me. There was part of me that knew that it would be the journey into the mountains for the spreading of Pete's remains, it would be in the Comeraghs where I would really be able to say goodbye.

The journey back to my children was punctuated with food stops and bottles of warm Heineken beer consumed in the car from the cocoon of my front passenger's chair. Once home, I quickly removed my mourning attire to appear normal again to my boys. Cahal was still ill, still curled in a ball, his tummy giving him severe trouble now. Eventually we managed to contact a health professional, who was able to advise us on how to get his bowels moving again. And once they started functioning, a week's worth of shit duly came out. Nothing could have better summed up the week I had just had.

With the funeral dispensed with, there was nothing else for it but to return home. Life went on, whether we liked it or not. I feared Pete's absence, but knew there was nothing else for it but to confront it head on.

Stepping through our front door back in Rostrevor, after less than a week away, it was the quietness that disturbed me at first. There was no greeting, no hugs or kisses, no questions about how our week had gone. Fortunately the kids quickly blasted this void away, bursting through the entrance in search of their long lost toys. The house was cold, the air drained of warmth. I turned on the heating, partly just to hear the hum of the boiler. It was also something to do, now that my role as Pete's carer was over.

There was nothing fresh in the fridge after being away for so long, so I had ordered a delivery from Tesco, to coincide with our own arrival home. I was also sick of eating sandwiches and drinking mugs of tea, things that are manufactured and consumed in vast quantities during Irish gatherings.

'Tesco man!' the boys shouted when they heard the reversing beep-beep-beep of the delivery van outside our home. It was so lovely to hear a snippet of normality after the week we had had. The boys swung the door open wide, letting all the heat out into the January night.

'Well hello, hello, hello,' Tesco man called like Santa, his arms laden with crates of food. Of course my kids thought he was bringing all manner of sweeties and goodies, not the staples of bread and milk I had ordered. They jumped around excitedly as he placed our food on the floor, ready to pounce on anything laden with sugar.

'So how was your Christmas?' Tesco man chimed off, placing some bananas and apples on our counter top.

'Oh, my husband died,' I said, without even thinking. 'He took his life two days after Christmas Day.'

Tesco man stood bolt upright, a carton of orange juice and a jar of raspberry jam balanced precariously in his palms. He looked like he was about to have a seizure.

'Oh shit, I'm sorry,' I said, reaching out to steady him, trying to retract my words.

I had spent every single minute of every day since Pete's disappearance and death speaking to people about those same events. Everyone who had spoken with me had done so already knowing exactly what had happened. This was the first time I had come face to face with someone who didn't know. I hadn't mentally prepared myself for what I would say to a stranger, hadn't constructed some sort of filter that would soften the blow. I didn't even realise it was possible to lie to Tesco man, to say we had a lovely Christmas, thanks so much for asking.

'I'm…I'm so sorry,' he said. 'I…'

'No, I'm sorry, it's my fault,' I replied. 'I just…I just thought everyone knew.'

I was right that everyone within the village was aware that there was a tragic death that had happened in the forest two days after Christmas. What I hadn't taken into account was life beyond Rostrevor had continued on as normal over the holidays.

Tesco man composed himself to finish the unpacking. He deducted from my total bill the substitutes I didn't want, but let me keep them anyway. 'Mind yourself,' he said as he left the house, shutting the door firmly behind him.

There was part of me that wanted to nail that door shut after him, to keep us safely confined within our world of grief. I wasn't quite yet ready to confront the world that was apparently still turning despite the fact that Pete was no longer part of it.

CHAPTER 8

REACHING OUT

I t was his absence that was the hardest part. Pete and I had been together for over eleven years. Even when Pete had gone on work trips, I had always felt his presence. He was a mere phone call away even when he was on the other side of the world. Now my phone lay there, silent.

My boys and I slept together in our double bed that first night home. We clung to each other in a bed made for two, our squashed-together bodies reminding us how much we needed each other now. More swallowed pills ensured I could sleep through their wriggling, dream-filled, night-time contortions.

I woke up the next morning, genuinely surprised to be still alive. When someone that close to you dies without warning, you start to believe that it'd be so easy for you to die too. Lying in the bed beside my two boys, I finally understood what was required of me. They needed me to stay alive. I needed to wake up that day, and the day after that, and to keep doing that until they didn't need me to rise.

I also had the advice from Henry, the local doctor, guiding me from that night. I was not to make any big decisions for the first year. I sensed that waking up on a daily basis would be a trivial enough plan to meet his approval. Hopefully then, after a year of waking up I would figure out what to do next with my shrunken, widowed, single-mothered existence.

After Pete passed away, so many people said to me, 'If you need anything, let us know.' I thanked them for their kindness and promised them I would. What they didn't understand was that I didn't know what to ask for. I was obviously broken, but didn't know what required fixing. Fortunately, one person knew what was needed, even before I did. I didn't even have to ask for her assistance.

When I had told my good friend Louise that Pete had died, the first thing she said was, 'I'm coming.' She lived in Kenya, a lifetime away, but from her home on the banks of Lake Victoria, she knew I needed her. She didn't even ask me if I wanted her to visit. She took that difficult decision-making out of my hands.

Louise couldn't make it in time for the funeral, but instinctively knew I'd want company in its aftermath. She arrived the day after we had reached home, swerving into our driveway with her tiny hire car from Dublin Airport. She rushed out of the car to embrace me. Bundled up in a thick coat, hat and gloves, I barely recognised her.

'I had to borrow these clothes from a neighbour,' she laughed, doing a quick twirl before hugging me tightly. Only true friends leave the warm tropics to see a friend in need who's in the depths of an Irish winter.

Together we cried tears of grief interspersed with tears of gratitude. We had not seen each other since my wedding day seven years previously, when she was my head bridesmaid.

'Come in, come in,' I said. 'Meet the kids.' Once inside, Louise dropped to her knees to speak to Aran and Cahal at their level. I explained to them that Louise had come all the way from Africa to see us.

'Have you brought presents?' they asked unashamedly.

'Of course I have,' Louise said, rummaging through her hand luggage. She produced beautiful wooden carvings of a lion, a hippo, a giraffe and a zebra. Aran and Cahal sprinted off with them, intent on playing a game of active jungle warfare with their newly acquired toys.

'So how are you?' Louise asked once we were alone.

Such an easy thing to ask, a nice opening question to start the ball rolling. I took a deep breath, but wasn't sure where to begin.

'Fine,' I said. 'Well, good I suppose, all things considered. I mean…' And then I burst out crying. Even a simple question like 'how are you' was just way too complicated for me. I felt endless despair that I didn't know how to answer it.

A bottle of wine was produced to help ease the conversation. I was just thankful that it wasn't another goddamn cup of tea. With the wine flowing, I talked and talked, repeating myself endlessly without even realising it. I went backwards and forwards, I rattled on, before welling up. I was a mess, but could be one in front of Louise.

Louise just listened, gave hugs when needed, and filled the void that was so obvious. She also was there when the police showed up.

'They can bring me to where Pete died,' I said to Louise once I had spoken with them. I could feel the blood draining from my face. 'Will you come with me and see it?'

Since Pete's death, my mind had been going over and over what could have possibly happened out there on that fateful day in December. Many of the scenarios were harrowing, concocted in my overactive imagination from a place of ignorance. I knew the only way I could set my mind straight was to understand exactly how Pete had died and to see where he had done the deed. Louise agreed to come with me.

Two policemen arrived in their four-by-four to transport us to the site. All I knew was that Pete died somewhere in the forest, but I just couldn't understand how. I needed to know where he had gone, what he had done. I hadn't been able to enter the forest since Pete's death, fearful that I would accidentally wander into the place where he had passed away.

They drove Louise and me on to the main forest trail, where Pete usually ran. Stopping close to the forest barrier, they showed me where they had found Pete's fluorescent jacket, the one he had left the house with that day. It was the one I was glad he had put on before leaving so he could be seen running in the dark.

'John found it when he was with the mountain rescue team,' they explained. 'It was neatly folded up at the base of the tree over there, like Pete had left some sort of marker.'

Pete had probably put it there to help us find him later. Though we drove on along the forest track, then double-backed up a side trail, Pete most likely took a shortcut and walked straight up the steep slope through the forest to his final resting place.

The police finally led me to the place where Pete's body had been found. It was a secluded place, a place through brambles and overturned trees where no one would normally go. It was like Pete didn't want to cause anyone any distress by accidentally finding his body on their morning walk or run. However, he also must have known that we would look for him, so left his jacket as a small sign to let us know where to start our search.

'There were no signs of distress or foul play,' the policeman explained as I stood at the place. 'I don't know if this makes it any easier, but the way he died, he would have gone quickly.' The policeman also showed me with great tact and respect signs of how they knew Pete was determined to end his life.

It sounded just like Pete. No fuss, just get the job done. And knowing how much depression had made him suffer by the end, I wasn't surprised that he had done it so decisively.

'He's not here,' I said, turning to Louise. 'I can't feel him here.'

I wasn't expecting to feel his presence. I hadn't gone there for that reason. I was just surprised at how emotionally empty I was in that place. In fact, I had not felt Pete's presence anywhere since the day he died. I had read how others who were bereaved had sensed their loved one close at times, had seen a sign coming from the other side. This was despite the fact that I believed in heaven, that I believed Pete was alive and well elsewhere. Despite this conviction, I still had received zero communication from my late husband.

My only way of explaining Pete's absence was that he was busy doing other things. He was probably chatting with Olga, a favourite work colleague of his who had passed away only a few months before after a brief but brutal battle with cancer. He was more than likely catching up with Chip, his former maverick tennis partner who had died in his sleep a few years before that. And knowing Pete, he was hanging out with Reggie, his beloved childhood dog, his pet who Pete was convinced had gained entry to doggie heaven thirty years beforehand. I figured that Pete was having too good a time to be bothering us with esoteric signs.

Though at the site I was calm and composed, I felt exhausted as soon as I returned home. I had used up all my energy in confronting the scene. But I was glad I had done so. It meant that my mind could no longer conjure up false, hurtful images and claim that they were true. I knew better now.

I had started to understand that the more I knew, the fewer surprises there were out there that could potentially be thrown at me. I was savvy enough to realise I couldn't anticipate all of them. Yet I resolved that, if anyone knew anything that helped shed light on Pete's life or death, I would welcome and listen to them.

Having seen where Pete had died and understood how he had done so, a switch flicked in my brain. I would never fully move on from what had happened, but I was desperate to inch forward, somehow. Maybe it was the sheer sadness of the situation that made me want to do something positive that could redress the hurt that had happened.

'Can you bring some of Pete's clothes back out to Kenya?' I asked Louise, once I had recomposed myself. 'It's just that, I'm not sure what I should do with them all.'

Pete had left a mountain of clothes behind when he went for his final run that day. It had never occurred to him that he was leaving me with the job of sorting through them and deciding what to do with them.

Louise suggested that a local football team in her hometown of Kisumu would take his running gear. So I found a large suitcase, one that Pete used on his frequent work trips, and started to load it up. Pete had won loads of t-shirts from all the road races he had done. I didn't remember Pete wearing half of them, so these were the first ones to go in. Pete had also bought new trainers in a discount store, in anticipation of when his own shoes would wear out. I threw these all into the suitcase, glad that they would go to good use.

As Pete's pile of clothes started to diminish, my packing began to slow. There was a sweat stained t-shirt I remembered Pete wearing when we lived in Vietnam. I held one of his jumpers a little longer, remembering how Pete would wear it while lounging around in front of the TV. I didn't want to be the type of person who kept all of Pete's belongings, who made a shrine to Pete, but I didn't want to toss out everything and later regret that I had no memories left of him.

Louise saw my reticence and swiftly intervened. 'That bag looks full,' she said, kneeling down and sliding shut its zip. 'I've a twenty-kilogram allowance anyhow, and I think that's at the limit.'

I looked on as she wheeled the bag down the corridor and out the door before dropping it in her car. She was being cruel to be kind, helping me move forward. She also recognised, however, the decisive moment when I could no longer bear parting with another of Pete's possessions. There was plenty of time to clear out Pete's stuff in the weeks and months ahead. Knowing the bag was going to people who would use and appreciate its contents eased the parting slightly.

'You've doing the right thing,' Louise said as she gave me another hug and let me cry again.

'I know,' I said. 'I know. It's just that, I keep on feeling like all I've got now is a quarter glass of milk.'

Louise moved me towards the sofa as I dried away my tears.

'There's an expression I can't stop thinking about. Don't cry over spilt milk,' I said, perching on the sofa's edge. 'But that's exactly what's happened. I had a full glass of milk, like everything in our life was going so well, and now the glass has been knocked over. All it took was a slight nudge. Now the milk is just lying there, totally wasted. I don't even have the energy to properly clean it up.' Louise nodded quietly as my words leaked out. She sat there in the awkward silence, waiting for me to speak. 'It's just that, seeing our boys, understanding how much Pete was loved, realising that I'm still here…I feel like the glass has been righted again, but only a quarter of the milk is left.'

It wasn't as if half the milk was gone, and that it depended on my perspective to say whether it was half full or half empty, as another saying went. It felt like three quarters of the glass were definitely, irrevocably drained from my life with Pete's untimely death.

'I look at all that's around me now and think, should I sit around and feel sad about the three quarters that I have just lost? Or do I get on with the quarter glass of milk that I still have, that is still with me now?'

Louise nodded wisely without saying a word. She knew me well enough to know what I would probably do with my lot.

My monologue was interrupted by the sound of the doorbell. I went to open the door to see Paddy our postman standing on our step. He was clutching a bunch of letters addressed to Aran and Cahal. Normally he would shove such post into our box and disappear, but this time it seemed as if he wanted to hand them over personally.

'I'm so sorry,' he said, looking down at the boys' letters, as if searching for his own words. 'My friend, he also went that way. Like Pete.'

'Ach, Paddy, I'm really sorry to hear that.'

'It's terrible, really terrible,' Paddy replied, 'Shouldn't be happening at all, but it is.'

'I know. It's such a waste.'

We were so lost in our respective sadness, unsure of how to articulate our own tragedies to each other. I never knew the local postal service could be so empathetic and caring.

Ever since that day, our postman Paddy has always kept a special eye out for my boys. He's given them a heads up when he has seen the Easter

Bunny on his rounds, personally placing chocolate eggs into our post box on the Bunny's behalf. He also updates them on Santa's exact whereabouts during the festive season.

'Does Postman Pat really know where Santa is?' my children would nervously ask me in the run up to Christmas Eve.

'Sure doesn't Paddy deliver cards and parcels for a living?' I'd say. 'Didn't you know Paddy is Santa's secret right-hand man?'

Louise was amazed to hear how even the postman was being so supportive. With such a strong community around me, she assured me that with time I'd be fine.

I wanted to repay Louise for helping me so much, before she flew back to Kenya. After some thought, it became clear how I could best assist.

'Want to go shoe shopping?' I said to her, once my gloom had lifted. When I said shoes, I of course didn't mean stilettos. Louise had shared with me her plans to run Kenya's Lewa Downs half marathon through the famous game reserve later that year. She needed some proper trail-running shoes to help her with her race plans.

We bundled the boys and ourselves into the car, and drove to the nearest running shop. Once there, Louise picked out trail shoes with proper grips that would speed her on her safari past all the wild animals that would be roaming freely on the route. The boys tried hard to contain their boredom at this shopping trip. It wasn't long before their cries reminded me that I hadn't really fed them properly that day. I couldn't remember either if there was any food left at home.

'Why don't we go to McDonald's?' Louise said, spying the yellow arches as we left the shop. I instinctively baulked at the idea of feeding my children junk food. I had successfully managed to avoid bringing them near that fast food chain since their birth.

'Old McDonald's!' Aran and Cahal cried with glee. Someone, somewhere had evidently introduced them already to the franchise, unbeknownst to me. I relented.

We did a drive-through to get chips and ice-cream, using the spacious boxes that had housed Louise's shoes to tip the chips into to help them cool down.

'Don't be afraid to make new memories,' Louise said to me, greedily licking her 99. 'Even if you never went to McDonald's when Pete was around, don't beat yourself up if you live your life slightly differently now.'

The idea of doing things differently than before petrified me. But if change meant small things like the occasional trips to McDonald's so that the kids didn't starve, then maybe that was achievable.

Louise could stay just two nights before she had to return home. She had listened, laughed, cried and consoled me during her short stay. She had held my hand as I stood at the edge of my grief abyss, showing me there was possibly another way round. She had not told me what to do. She had merely steadied me so that I would be able to make decisions going forward.

It was only as she was about to leave that she gave me parting advice.

'Be careful with those pills,' she said. 'I know you're using them to help you sleep, but they're really addictive. Try to get yourself off them as soon as you can.' The idea of parting with my pills felt like going through yet another loss, but I took her advice and thanked her for it. She was probably right.

Days later, Louise sent me photos of happy Kenyans wearing Pete's sporting gear. Seeing their expressions, it was clear that I had made the right decision to part with some of Pete's belongings.

It wasn't just Louise who had worked out what I needed before I knew it myself. Some of Pete's work colleagues also rushed to my aid without me even signalling for help.

With Pete being the main breadwinner and an accountant by profession, I had always left the household accounts in his more than competent hands. Now that he was gone, I had no clue about the state of our finances. The horrible reality of suicide is that Pete walked out of the house without giving me a final debrief. He didn't leave me a note, didn't sit me down and tell me where monies were or what would be due on his death.

After he died, official looking letters had come in the post addressed to Pete. I had left them all unopened. I was so used to receiving bad news at that stage that I feared discovering something in those envelopes that I couldn't handle. Three of Pete's colleagues, lawyers and accountants by trade, figured that I was probably drowning in all the administrative tasks that were required of me. So they arrived at my door one evening, took notes of what little I knew, then literally walked out the door carrying Pete's filing cabinet and laptop.

'Don't worry,' they said. 'We'll sort it out.'

It was a move that I would be forever grateful for. It meant there was one less thing for me to worry about, allowing me to concentrate on restoring some sort of normality for my boys and me.

CHAPTER 9

CAIRNUARY

Before I knew it, Monday morning had swung by and schools were open again after the Christmas break. I had emailed Aran's school and Cahal's playgroup during the holidays to let them know what had happened. I had spoken with Aran's headmaster directly, who had called to offer his condolences. I had explained to him what Aran understood; that his Daddy had been sick and that the doctors couldn't make him better; that his Daddy was now safely in heaven. To avoid any confusion, I wanted our messages at home and school to be consistent.

The teachers at Cahal's playgroup had not replied to my note. I assumed they hadn't picked up the message, so would wait to speak to them directly once the playgroup had opened.

Standing outside playgroup with Cahal, I suddenly wondered if sending the boys back to school so soon was a good idea. Other parents had also gathered round with their three-year-olds, waiting for the doors to open. I wasn't sure if the lack of chat between us all was because of what had happened. Were they avoiding eye contact with me because they knew of our yuletide tragedy but didn't know what to say? Did they pity my poor son, now that he was one step closer to becoming a full-blown orphan? Or did they have no idea of what had happened and were just bleary eyed from the first early morning start after the holidays? I felt acutely embarrassed, unsure of what to do. I averted my gaze, making myself inconspicuously small by crouching down and wrapping my arms tightly around Cahal, hoping his presence would protect me from our new complicated reality.

My relief was palpable when I heard the lock turn to let the children in. Cahal sprinted out of my arms, intent on getting first dibs on his favourite toys that he'd not seen in two weeks. I stepped in after him to see the teachers clearly distraught.

'I'm not sure you know, if you saw…my email. The one I sent.'

The head teacher gently led me aside, away from my stuttering sentences, and into the privacy of their office. 'I'm so sorry,' she said. 'We just got the email this morning. I'm so sorry for your loss.'

We were both in uncharted territory now, trying to work out what to do next. I thought it would best if I offered some suggestions.

'I just thought it was best to get Cahal back into a routine,' I said. 'He's doing okay, all things considered.' I explained to her what I had told Cahal, why his Daddy was no longer there. 'But I can bring him back home with me if you think best.'

'No, no,' she replied. 'We'll keep an eye on him here. If we've any worries, I promise we'll call you.'

I peeked around the playgroup's door as I was leaving to see if Cahal was doing okay. I saw him busy scooping sand into a plastic bulldozer that he was intent on driving to the other end of the play-tray. It was like nothing had happened in the intervening weeks since he was last at playgroup, when they closed the term with the nativity play that his Daddy had attended.

It quickly dawned on me that bringing Cahal back to familiar faces, allowing him to be with his friends and teachers was the right thing to do. He was too young to sit around depressed, to question why all this had happened to him. He just needed to slot back into what he did best, which was to play and learn and have fun.

The day before the return to school, Henry, our local doctor, had texted me inviting me on a walk up Slieve Martin, the mountain that overlooks Rostrevor village. He was going up there anyway as part of something known as 'Cairnuary'. I replied, saying I'd join him once I had dropped the kids off. So straight after leaving Cahal to playgroup, I drove to the local forestry office to wait for Henry there.

Cairnuary is a challenge that Henry had dreamed up a few years before-hand. It had started out as a plan with a couple of his mates to climb to the cairn on top of Slieve Martin in time for New Year's sunrise. It was a way of kick-starting their year with a large helping of exercise and a good dose of fresh air. Arriving back at the forestry office at sea level, Henry felt great. He soon worked out that if he made his way to the 485-meter high summit every day for the entire month of January, he'd have climbed a height greater than Everest. So for the rest of January, Henry made a daily visit to the cairn on the top of Slieve Martin. The Cairn-uary challenge was born.

It did Henry so much good that he started selling the challenge at work, at his GP's office. He'd open his door at the start of the year to see his wait-ing room full of people. January was a particularly hard month for many. He could see that most of them were overweight, had high blood pressure, were suffering from diabetes. Many of them felt depressed. The majority wanted him to write them a prescription. Instead Henry prescribed them Cairnuary. For those with mild to moderate depression, his treatment plan was based on evidence that suggested that an hour's daily exercise can be just as effective as medication.

Henry was already at the forestry office with his springer spaniels as I pulled up in my car. With a busy doctor's schedule ahead of him, he was raring to get going, to fit his daily cairn visit in. I had been to the top of Slieve Martin many a time on mountain runs, so I knew it would take around an hour to walk it. We immediately set off without formality, Henry's dogs leading the way.

'Thanks for visiting me after Pete died,' I said immediately, cutting to the chase. 'Your advice was direct, to say the least, but it was a real help.'

'I wasn't looking forward to that visit,' Henry replied. 'But I knew I couldn't candy coat it. How are you keeping now?'

Maybe it had been the fact that I had managed to wake up that day and successfully gotten us all out of bed. Perhaps it was because we had all got dressed and fed and out the door on time. Was it because I had spent quality time speaking with Louise about my thoughts and feelings over the previous days, which had helped me to start processing them? Or was it because so many people had said we were in their thoughts and prayers that I felt them gently carrying me? Whatever the reason, I was able to tell my local doctor that, right there and then, I was keeping relatively well.

I was well aware that there are official stages to the grieving process. First denial, then anger, followed by bargaining, depression and acceptance. The day Pete went missing was my denial stage, step one of the cycle. Somehow I had seemingly skipped steps two and three, the anger or bargaining bits. Yes, I had been depressed since Pete's passing, at times intensely sad and distinctly overwhelmed, but this fourth stage seemingly came and went. That morning as I climbed towards the cairn with Henry, I felt that I had started to accept the reality of Pete's death; that I had arrived at the fifth and final acceptance stage. It meant that I was probably done with the whole grieving process, thank you very much.

I was, of course, still in deep shock. It was probably also pride, verging on sheer stupidity, that made me think that I had successfully passed through the grieving cycle and already graduated. Little did I know that I was going to cover all the steps, just in a very different order than to the one I had read on the Internet.

'This might sound horrible,' I continued, 'but I'm just glad Pete is at peace now.'

'Living with a depressed person isn't easy,' Henry said, as we began to climb the rocky path that ran parallel to Kilbroney River. 'They can't see all the good things they have. They tend to overemphasise the bad stuff.' I nodded silently, wondering how he knew these things about Pete's depressed behaviour that I hadn't dared divulge to others while he was still alive? All along, I thought it was I who was misreading what Pete thought was so obvious through the lens of his mental illness.

Excited barks from Henry's dogs reminded me not to let my thoughts slow us down. They forced me to keep pace as we journeyed upward through the thick forest. 'You have to remember, Pete made his own decision to end his life,' Henry continued. 'There's nothing you could have done about it.'

I had started to count the number of times I cried per day and keep a running tally. That Monday I had successfully managed not to shed a single tear, even outside Cahal's playgroup. But on hearing a medical professional telling me that Pete's suicide was not my fault, I could feel my throat clogging up. Hearing that someone understood my situation and didn't blame me made me feel relieved yet simultaneously sad.

'You've still a way to go,' Henry continued. 'But the bereaved need closure. Bereavement is like a deep wound. It takes time, and although it will heal, a scar will be left in its place.'

I wondered how long it would take my scar to form. It had been less than two weeks since Pete's death, still very much early days. What I really wanted to know from this doctor was what treatment was required. How exactly was I meant to steer my healing process so my wound didn't become infected with bitterness, anger and regret?

I was desperate for a plan. I wanted a clear outline of what to expect and when. When I struggled with pregnancy, knowing that it would be all over in nine months and I'd have a baby at the end allowed me count down the weeks. When I was competing, a training schedule showing me what I needed to do on a daily basis to achieve that elusive podium place come race day.

Henry was hesitant to tell me what to do. The grieving process is so individual, so personal, so fraught with caveats and exceptions that he couldn't prescribe me anything. Fortunately an elderly man descending through the forest in our direction interrupted my demands for a carefully constructed care plan.

'Howaya Henry?' he said, hobbling towards us.

'I see you're getting out and about Malachy,' Henry said.

'Och, sure, got to keep moving, you know yerself,' Malachy replied. 'I must come and see you about my arthritis though.'

'Make an appointment, Malachy,' Henry shouted without missing a step, unwilling to deliver consultations on the wooded slopes. 'I'll see you at the surgery.'

We left the river to walk a short distance through the top car park, towards the track known locally as the zigzags.

'There's a patient of mine who's been quite ill, in fact has had surgeries on both her feet,' Henry explained. 'She shouldn't really be doing Cairnuary, I think it's a bit too much for her, but she still insists on driving every day to this car park and doing the second half of the mountain section to the cairn.'

'Fair play,' I said, as I watched mountain bikers unloading their two-wheeled steeds from the back of parked vans, ready to hit the trails that littered this side of the mountain. I'd always loved how in Rostrevor there are always people out and about doing some sort of exercise.

'It's pretty amazing seeing what people get out of doing it,' Henry continued. 'A lot of my patients lose weight, get fitter both mentally and physically. What's most impressive though is seeing improvements in their self-esteem.' It would be hard not to think you're ace if you're able to force yourself to go out every day in the month of January in the dark, rain and cold to climb a big mountain. Doing something like that takes real self-discipline.

I had indeed seen online how people had become addicted to Cairnuary. The rule was that, when you got to the summit, you took a selfie and posted it on the Facebook group. Each photo was soon after accompanied by heart-warming likes and positive comments from other Cairnuary stalwarts.

Henry and I continued on up the zigzags, the path steepening with every step. I breathed in the cold January forest air, glad to be outside again. It had never struck me before how much mourning in Ireland takes place indoors.

'Wooww, watch out below,' I suddenly heard, voices shouted from above. I looked up to see three female friends from the village hurtling down the path.

'What's the rush?' I shouted as they threw themselves down the hill.

'Doing catch-up!' one shouted. 'Missed our cairns over the weekend, so gotta do three today.' I turned to Henry, about to question what magical spell he had cast on Rostrevor to make people go up and down the mountain not once, not twice, but three times in a day.

'Some people really like to get in their thirty-one cairn trips,' he explained, as if reading my thoughts. 'And anyhow, a bit of tiredness and suffering isn't a bad thing. They'll probably feel it tomorrow though,' the sadist in Henry slipping out momentarily.

Henry and I slowly emerged from the pine forest, leaving the zigzags behind to begin the final short ascent up to Slieve Martin's summit. The vastness of Carlingford Lough stretched out below us, colliding with the impressive Cooley Mountains rising from their depths. It was as if the legendary giant Fionn Mac Cumhaill himself had gorged the land out with his own bare hands, dumping the darkened earth on the lough's banks to form this ragged knuckle-shaped mountain range. I always loved how standing high on mountainsides always made me feel so small and insignificant.

Walking up towards the cairn, we met more and more people descending from the summit, each one respectfully greeting Henry in turn.

'I think one of the best things that has happened thanks to Cairnuary is the community that has formed,' Henry said, brushing aside his evident celebrity status. 'People tend to bump into the same people doing the hike each day, whether it's stay-at-home parents going out in the morning or nine-to-five workers fitting it in in the evening. Then on the last weekend, we organise a community cairn when everyone hikes up together.'

Just as the slope tailed off, the stone pillar came into sight. Henry grabbed a quick selfie to prove his ascent, before quickly turning around to commence our return journey.

I couldn't help wondering whether I should do Cairnuary that year, in remembrance of Pete. I could see the multiple benefits reaped by those who committed to the challenge. But there was part of me that wasn't ready to reflect. Happy memories of Pete were still so mixed up with the horrific reality of his illness and of how bruised and battered Pete was by the end.

I needed to do something to make me go forward as opposed to looking back. This wasn't just for my own sanity, but because my boys demanded it. They were growing up, concerned with the here and now, and moving relentlessly forward, whether I liked it or not. I also needed to do the same, at least initially, to keep my diminished family intact.

CHAPTER 10

TRAINING TIREDNESS

I picked the boys up from playgroup and school once they had finished their respective days. Both sets of teachers informed me the boys had happily slotted back into their old routines, news I gratefully received. Aran's primary school teacher in particular took me aside to share how Aran's day had gone.

'Aran did really well in school today,' his teacher told me. 'He stood up in front of his class and told them that his Daddy was sick, and that over Christmas he died.' I looked down at Aran, who was holding on to my hand, oblivious to my amazement.

'Yeah, and we all said a prayer for Daddy,' Aran chimed in from below, as if this classroom activity was the most normal thing in the world. I tightened my grip, pride soaring within me as I witnessed my child coping so well. It seemed like Aran and Cahal were processing Pete's death better than most of the adults I knew.

Despite my children's unquestioning attitude, I had already started to seek out counselling for our family. I was aware that, as they both got older, questions would arise from them using more pertinent words like 'where' and 'why' did Daddy die. I needed to be prepared with age-appropriate answers, as well as have professional services lined up in case I had no idea how to reply.

In the interim, I began receiving my own counselling support to help me through those initial days. When I spoke to my counsellor about my children, she gave me booklets to help Aran and Cahal come to terms with what had happened. Their pages listed the many thoughts and feelings that we were probably having, everything from numbness, shock and disbelief to guilt, anger and even relief. They warned me that our family could feel a sense of rejection and betrayal. Later there could be shame and blame. It was comforting to know that these reactions were in no way out of the ordinary.

The pages also advised me on how to begin explaining the concept of suicide to my children. Inside there were drawings done by other kids who were coming to terms with their own loss, art therapy apparently being one of the ways that helps children process their thoughts. I struggled to look at a coloured-in sketch of a person hanging from a ceiling drawn by a thirteen-year old son. Even if producing such pictures proved profoundly helpful, I wasn't ready to see Aran or Cahal drawing such a graphic image of their dad.

As I searched to move forward, there were a few things that helped me immensely during those early days of bereavement. Being fed was one of them. My mind was so busy dealing with pressing issues, I kept forgetting to cook or eat. From the roast chicken and coleslaw brought over the night of Pete's death by a friend, to the thick stew and warm potatoes served up the day after the funeral, I still remember those meals being placed in front of me without my asking. I am forever grateful for being given food during those early days.

John and Nina, our former neighbours, had also noted my ever-diminishing size resulting from my forgetfulness. They knew that, what with all the exercise I normally did, I didn't have much more fat to lose. So they invited the boys and I over for a lavish dinner soon after our return in an attempt to restore my waistline. The food was magnificent, soft roast lamb with crisp potatoes and thick gravy accompanied by perfectly sautéed greens. An equally fattening and sugary dessert, drenched in lashings of ice cream, followed this.

I, however, was less interested in the food than the bottle of French wine that accompanied it. John poured me a large glass, which slipped down my throat with remarkable ease. He barely batted an eyelid as he refilled my glass, which I proceeded to demolish as well.

I had barely drunk alcohol since having children. I was either breast-feeding, so didn't want to inebriate my babies, or was in serious training mode. My coach had told me to cut it out, but I had managed to hone my intake down to a very occasional glass, and only if I was not racing.

The problem was that, right then, I found drinking really helped. By the end of most days, my head was bulging with stressful thoughts that I couldn't shake. A glass of wine or a bottle of beer was the easiest way of calming them. I just made sure I remained below the legal limit so I'd be able to drive the children to hospital if anything catastrophic happened them. It wasn't like, if one of them had an accident, there was a spare sober parent on call in the house to transport them.

Having dinner with John and Nina meant that, if the kids hurt themselves under their roof, one of them could drive the casualty to A&E on my behalf. It was the first time in a long time that I could stop being solely responsible. I was starting to understand why the single parents I knew looked permanently under siege.

'So how are things going?' Nina asked me, as I started to nurse a third glass of red. Unfortunately my drinking had loosened the lock on the control gates I had successfully installed after Pete's death. The anger part of my grieving cycle was bubbling behind them, ready to burst forth if and when a weakness appeared in this defence.

'I'm really fucked off that Pete pissed off,' I said, startling myself with my reply. That was before I caught the shocked reaction plastered across Nina's face. 'I'm so sorry,' I muttered, hanging my head with guilt. I felt I shouldn't have said those words even though I felt better after letting them out.

In addition to drinking, swearing had become another one of my tried and tested therapeutic ways of dealing with my grief. They were not officially sanctioned ways by any means; indeed most bereavement websites recommended techniques like meditation instead.

I had heard, however, that the first year after a death is the hardest because it is exactly that – a year of firsts. There's the first time you'll celebrate their birthday, Valentine's day, your wedding anniversary, Christmas, Easter, your own birthday without them there. If drinking and swearing were going to help me get through that first year, I didn't care if these techniques were detrimental in other more long-term ways.

Things got better when I actually ate my dinner, and soaked up some of the alcohol I had consumed.

The good thing about John and Nina was that conversations could wander comfortably between topics without being stilted or banal. One thing I had in common with Nina was that she was also an off-road runner, having competed in many trail ultra-marathons around the globe. She was more interested in pre-marked routes on defined paths than I, so we had never actually raced each other. Our love of testing ourselves to the limit on the run was, however, our common ground.

'Have you been able to get out and train?' Nina asked me, once our plates had been cleared away.

'Not really,' I replied. 'I ran a bit just before Pete's funeral, but that didn't go so well.' I told her what had happened in Waterford, how the solitude of running had allowed room for an all out panic attack.

'Maybe when things settle down, it might help to get back out there,' she replied. She told me of times she had gone through, when things were tough, that training was the last thing on her mind. However she also knew that having a goal, like a race she wanted to do, had pulled her through such moments.

The only thing was that training had already taken more and more of a back seat during the preceding months, when Pete's condition had worsened. During the initial days when Pete wasn't that sick, I had continued to turn up to races I had pre-entered. I was worried about leaving Pete at home alone, to mind the kids, but he had always assured me that everything would be fine in my absence. It all came to head when I ran the Mourne Mountain Marathon in September of that year, a two-day race with an overnight mountain camp. The race itself took place nearby, so I knew I would never be more than a thirty-minute drive away from home if needed. I wanted to race hard, so I opted to run without the weight of a phone in my rucksack, instead scribbling Pete's number on my map in permanent marker. I knew there would be someone in one of the non-competitive categories who would lend me their mobile that evening for a quick call home.

When I spoke with Pete from camp that evening, he convinced me everything was fine. We chatted briefly about the race. I shared with him how tough the course and the conditions had been before promising I'd be home as quickly as I could the next day. When I returned home, Pete eventually admitted to me that all had not gone well. Something had happened while I was away, something his mind interpreted to mean that he was under attack. It was the first indication of the terrifying paranoia that would increasingly manifest itself until his death.

Though I abandoned any thoughts of racing after that incident, I hoped I would at least keep my fitness up. I believed that keeping active would help me cope with having two boisterous children and a poorly husband at home.

Pete didn't want me to tell others that he was sick, but I could not agree to keep silent when it came to speaking with my coach, Eamonn. I felt like I had no choice but to inform him that all was not well in my life. It was obvious, anyhow, by the way I was skipping sessions, missing sleep and struggling to hit training heart rates that something was up.

Eamonn heard what I was saying and was extremely understanding. He agreed to scale back my training plan to keep me ticking over. Even this, however, failed to work. He'd give me a gentle bike ride to do with no high-power efforts involved. I'd be no sooner out of the house, pedalling away, than my brain would take over, bombarding me with unruly thoughts. I had assumed that gentle exercise would become my de-stressor, but all it did was provide an open mic for the worries and anxieties I had haphazardly stuffed away. Once my body was pre-occupied with physical exercise, all my stresses would shift to the forefront of my mind.

'How is Pete going to get better? Will he get better? Why isn't he getting better? What if he never gets better? What will you do then?' These questions, to which I had no answers, went around and around in circles.

It was terrifying.

It meant that I had to go back to Eamonn to ask for more punishing sessions. If I had intervals to do, at least my brain was silenced as I pushed myself hard, my legs screaming out so loud that they drowned out my thoughts. At the end of the interval, I could busy myself with counting down the seconds before I had to push myself again. Lung-busting intervals helped stop the rumination, only to soon find that my body couldn't physically cope.

There was a book on training I had once seen that had tried to explain stress. There are so many different pressures in our lives, both positive and negative, such as family, illness, work and relationships. Training is another strain we can add to that mix. The stress of Pete's illness, of not being allowed to tell others what was going on, of looking after our two children who were starting to notice things were not right, the worries about our future and how we would cope; putting training on top of all of these only caused me to break. I was tired, so tired, both mentally and physically. Nothing I did to try and manage the situation seemed to work.

With Pete's death, I was hesitant to turn to training as a miracle cure, when it had failed me so miserably just when I had needed it the most. So I spoke honestly and openly with Eamonn and explained my dilemma. I apologised again and again for my inability to run or bike. I told him it was probably best I signed off for a while. I refrained from informing him that I was going to take up drinking and swearing as my way of coping with my lot.

'Just take it slowly,' Eamonn said reassuringly. 'You've been through a massive trauma. Let's work together, just take this day by day and see what happens.'

With no pressure from Eamonn to get back out there, I felt a little better. It was like he gave me permission to stop worrying about it all. After working with him for over five years, I also trusted him profoundly. Instead of harping on about training, Eamonn instead went back to basics and reminded me about the meds. I needed to get off the sleeping tablets. With his support, I went cold turkey, and with the assistance of the occasional herbal remedy, I was able to start sleeping eight to nine hours a night.

These long sleeps were instrumental in making me a little saner and helped me cope a bit more. Slowly Eamonn started slotting training suggestions into my training plan. When I looked at them, however, I instinctively knew I wasn't ready. He'd give me an easy run outside, but I'd replace it that day with a short session of stretching. A bike session I substituted with an easy hike with a friend. Where before Eamonn would have questioned my switching around of sessions, this time around he commended me for the slightest effort made.

The activity that frightened me most at that time was getting back on my bike and riding it outside. My ruminations about Pete's fate were now replaced with a vivid awareness of how dangerous road cycling was. I knew the roads around Rostrevor were relatively safe, yet I had become convinced that an errant driver would knock me down while on a spin and that my children would be left forever parent-less.

I found whatever excuse I could to ride my bike indoors. I blamed the weather for being too cold, too icy, too windy, too inclement to cycle outside. I proclaimed that I had no childcare available that day, so had to go on my biking rollers so as to keep an eye on the kids. In an effort to beat the boredom of indoor pedalling, I started to listen to podcasts during my training. It was a solution that worked surprisingly well. I listened to anything and everything, from *Desert Island Disks* to former Labour leader Ed Miliband's *Reasons to be Cheerful*. I'd catch up on Irish news with Today FM's Matt Cooper before dipping my toe into Radio 4's *Women's Hour* podcast. It was wonderfully distracting, to realise there was a world out there full of ideas and people and situations that didn't involve widowhood or single-parenting or grief.

I brought my podcasts along with me when Eamonn prescribed me sessions of indoor rowing. They broke the monotony of pushing and pulling and getting nowhere that only indoor rowers can bestow. Getting back on the indoor rower also inadvertently helped me move forward in a way that I didn't expect.

I had a habit of taking off my rings when getting on to the machine. The metal would press hard into my fingers and hurt them from the very first stroke, so there was no way I could wear such jewellery while rowing. One day I slid off my rings as normal and placed them on a nearby counter, with the usual intention of replacing them once I was done. Only that, when I had finished my session that day, I was hit with a dilemma I had been totally blind to thus far. I saw my wedding ring sitting there on the counter, its perfect shape and form willing me to put it back on my finger like I usually did, in remembrance of Pete and our love. I knew, however, that my reality was now different. Sliding it back on to my hand felt like I would be living a perpetual lie. I was no longer married, something even my car insurance renewal had reminded me lately when they forced me to select from the drop-down window 'widowed' as my marital status. I couldn't pretend anymore.

In the weeks that followed, my hand balked at my wedding ring's absence. The thin band of white skin surrounded by tan lines on my fourth finger, the obvious indent from where the ring had once nestled snugly, these were stark reminders that it was gone. But despite my hand's objections, I knew my wedding ring was now in the right place, tucked away safely with Pete's. They were at least reunited, even though Pete and I were apart.

Making small yet decisive moves like this gave me the confidence to edge forward in other ways. I hadn't returned to the forest since the day the policemen brought me there, to show me where Pete had died. I needed to reclaim the forest again, to make it a safe place for me to run once more. I couldn't bear the idea of retracing Pete's steps; to take the same route he did the day he went missing. So I purposefully set off in the opposite direction, with the intention of turning around if it all got too much.

As I neared the section of forest where Pete had carefully left his high-vis jacket, I started to slow my pace. It was a section of the Mourne Way that both Pete and I had agreed during happier times was one of the prettiest parts. The trees on either side of the path stood tall and straight. In between their roots, thick green moss gently covered its rolling forest floor. Somehow I felt safe under the protective canopy the tree branches wove overhead.

I started to think; maybe it was okay that Pete had been in such a tranquil area when depression forced his hand. Maybe it was good that he at least got to see this beautiful place before he finally closed his eyes. Despite these comforting thoughts, I knew I could not leave the forest in limbo. I was still here, I was still alive, and I wanted to be able to run through these woods until the day I also died. And so I ran, and ran, past the tree that Pete had marked and out into the open, knowing that in doing so I could return to that place once more.

Despite making inroads into having a training routine again, the idea of using my fitness to race continued to traumatise me. Every time I thought about competing, my stomach lurched. I couldn't bear the idea of pushing myself to the limit when I was still at a stage where getting through the day was a major daily feat.

Losing this desire to race petrified me. For the past five years, I had competed all around the country and had been crowned Irish Adventure Racing Champion three times. It was such a fundamental part of who I was that I couldn't help worrying that I had been irrevocably changed by the bereavement I had suffered. When I voiced this concern with Eamonn, he put me at ease. 'Forget about racing,' he said. He reminded me to focus on just the day to day, and when the time was right, it would happen. It was another conversation that helped put my mind at ease. Sometimes just voicing the things that were freaking me out helped show me how they really weren't a big deal.

Soon after that, it became clear I could put the training I was doing to a much better use. I needed to return to the mountainside once more, but this time armed with hiking boots.

CHAPTER 11

EXPEDITION

At the time of Pete's death, I had already completed two out of the three weekends that were part of my Mountain Leader award training. The third and final weekend was scheduled to take place a fortnight after his funeral. I wasn't sure what to do. Part of me felt that I was meant to shut myself away; to dress all in black, enter a period of mourning while playing soulful dirges in a darkened room. The other part of me felt I had to put my head down and plough on regardless, that life was shit, but you had no choice but to just get on with it.

I called the Tollymore National Outdoor Centre reception to make discreet enquiries. Was there any chance the final training weekend would be delayed if there was, say, adverse weather? If I did miss the weekend, when would the course be available again? I frowned when I heard it would take a major snowstorm coupled with a freak earthquake to prevent the tutors from heading out. It would be at least another couple of months before the training would be repeated.

I sat and thought long and hard about what I should do. Eventually I called the person in charge and came clean about my dilemma. Whether I liked it or not, news of my bereavement had already infiltrated through to parts of the outdoor community. Calling out local mountain rescue had helped ensure that.

I didn't need to go into great detail. He had already heard of my loss.

'I'll totally understand if you think this is a bad idea,' I said. 'But if it's okay with you, I'd like to attend the final training weekend.' I explained to him that I wanted to finish the course with my fellow trainees, people who I felt comfortable with after the two short weekends we'd spent together. Finishing the training was a major pre-requisite when signing up for the award's assessment. I wanted to get on with preparing for that. 'I promise I'll hike out if it gets too much,' I said, hoping this caveat would be enough to convince him to allow me to go ahead.

I'm not sure if it was just because he appreciated the frankness of my forewarning, but he agreed that, if I felt up for it, then he was fine for me to join.

I knew the final weekend was not, however, going to be a walk in the park. It was billed as the hardest part of the course, the infamous expedition weekend. We were to pack everything we needed for two days in the mountains. Though we had to bring a tent, mat and sleeping bag along, opportunities for sleep would be sparse. Where on previous sessions we had perfected our navigation in broad daylight, this time it was all about heading out to spend most of the night navigating in the pitch dark. If there were the slightest weaknesses in the way we used our maps and compasses, this would be when they would be ruthlessly exposed.

Since the previous trainings, I had fortunately made in-roads in improving my clothing. I had contacted friends in mountain rescue who were used to standing around for hours in the worst of conditions while rescuing poor unfortunates. They recommended a host of fail-proof brands that would keep me warm and dry no matter the weather. I used the opportunity of the Christmas sales to buy a better jacket, warmer layers and impenetrable waterproofs. At least I'd not get cold while I got hopelessly lost in the dark.

It was only when I pulled out my camping equipment that I knew I had so much more to do. I had only the lightest of equipment, gear that was the bare minimum to get me through an ultra mountain race. My tent had pegs the size of toothpicks, with no guy-lines to tie it down. It had just about stood up to a mild autumnal breeze during the previous Mourne Mountain Marathon. I wasn't sure if it would remain erect in mid-January when the weekend's weather forecast was already predicting gale-force winds. With no time to upgrade, I decided to just go out there, inspect the camping equipment all the seasoned rock climbers and hill walkers in my group were using, and then buy new gear once the course was over.

There's no easy way to let people know your husband has died. Just like I discovered when informing Tesco man how my Christmas had gone, I still wasn't sure of the best way of letting my fellow trainees know of my recent loss. I had to let them know, however, in case they wondered why I was quieter, thinner, more distracted than before. I also wanted to forewarn them in case it all became too much and they saw me turning around in the middle of the night and hiking out towards the nearest road.

All I knew was, whatever I said, I wasn't to use the term 'commit suicide'. Apparently this term harkened back to the olden days when such an act was treated as a crime. I had also grown up being taught that suicide was a sin, with those doing so being consigned to hell because of their outright rejection of the life God had given them. Even though saying someone had 'committed suicide' was out-dated and insensitive, I had to constantly remind myself not to use the phrase.

When I informed the other trainees that, since I last saw them, my husband had 'died by suicide', they immediately expressed their regret. By then I had gotten better at accepting condolences, and had learned that if I moved the conversation swiftly on to another topic, everyone appreciated it. Switching to talk about how nervous we all were about the expedition made us all feel infinitely more at ease.

'Is that your rucksack?' Caris asked me as we started to make moves towards the bus. She placed her own bag beside it, illustrating how mine was half the size. While she started stressing that she had brought too much, I was concerned that I had brought too little. Only time on the mountain would ultimately prove who was best prepared.

As soon as we were dropped off at Dunnywater, on the southern side of the Mourne Mountains, I was amazed at how quickly I eased into the day. Tuning into the mountains and their corresponding maps was just like listening to podcasts on the indoor rower. It prevented me thinking about past events or future impasses. It just forced me to concentrate on the here and now, and the only job I had to do right then was make sure I didn't mess up my map reading.

We spent the day trawling the slopes around Long Seefin, then over towards Rocky Mountain. At this stage of proceedings, navigating us to the correct place was no longer good enough. When I was given a leg to lead, I soon realised that part of the journey meant crossing the Mourne Wall. This would have been fine around more popular areas, where there are numerous stiles positioned at key points to help climb over the seven-foot wall. Around this area of the southern Mournes that is less popular with walkers, the only stile available involved a considerable detour, something I knew everyone would grumble about. The wall had also undergone extensive repairs, so there were no tumbled-down gaps I could sneak us through.

Instead I was faced with this stone edifice that I had to get us up and over, in tandem with our heavy packs. If anyone fell or hurt themselves getting over this obstacle, it would be an immediate black mark against me in the instructor's book.

When faced with the Mourne Wall during mountain-running races, the rule is typically every man and woman for themselves. Even when I've raced in a team with taller, more agile males than myself, men who could leap over the wall in a single stride, none of them would ever have considered stopping to give me a hand up. I think they were worried they'd be later accused of singling me out for being a weaker female. Sometimes the gender equality, often celebrated within mountain-running circles, is really annoying.

I had no choice but to ask our instructor the best way of getting us over the wall in one piece. 'Everyone needs to take off their packs,' he said. 'Then Moire, why don't you sit on the top slab?' I did as he suggested, before he ordered the packs to be handed to me one-by-one. I then lowered them down safely on the other side. The group then clambered over the wall, pack and incident-free.

Once safely back on terra firma, the whole manoeuvre was debriefed. Should someone have spotted people from the ground in case they misplaced their foot and fell backwards off the wall? Should I have brought someone to sit on top with me to help hoist people up? It all seemed so convoluted, yet I could see our instructor's point. Safety was paramount, especially when the slightest fall could have far-reaching implications in the middle of the mountains. I could see that my gung-ho days of racing, where taking safety precautions equated lost time and potential slippage down the race rankings, would be frowned upon in present company.

We continued to hike over to the rocky buttress that is Hare's Castle, before descending into the sweeping Annalong Valley. On a bend in its river, we set up camp. Already I could feel the wind that had been forecast picking up. I pushed in my miniature tent pegs and prayed that they would hold fast for the night.

'Everyone be ready with head-torches, maps and compasses to head out at 7 pm.' These were our instructor's parting words to us as we all scurried into our respective tents to eat and rest before then. With it being mid-January, it was already dark by 5 pm. I lay in my tent in the dark, with the wind battering my flysheet, wondering what the hell I was doing. 'Camping out in wintery, stormy conditions' hadn't been listed on the worldwide web as a recommended way of grieving.

According to mountain runners, the standard rule about night navigation is that you should avoid it all costs. If you're in a race that continues throughout the night and you're allowed to decide your own route, the key is making sure you're not in the middle of the mountains when it's dark. The terrain is too indistinct. It's so easy to make mistakes. You have to slow down and check, check, check your compass, which loses you precious time. The trick is planning your route so that, as soon as night falls, you're on roads or unmistakable tracks. Now I was being asked to do something I was told never to do. I was purposely breaking a fundamental ultra-mountain-running rule.

Because I had avoided opportunities to practise night navigation for over a decade, I had very little experience. I had also inadvertently developed a profound phobia of what I was about to do. It meant, as I emerged from my tent at 7 pm, I was totally terrified. I was greeted by a huddle of brightly lit head-torches that had already formed outside. I walked towards the group to shelter from the wind that was battering us all. Even when our instructor showed up, I could see from everyone's body language that we all wanted this session quickly over and done with.

Fortunately I had had a chance to rectify my pacing counts in the intervening weeks. This was going to prove key in making sure I knew where I was by helping me calculate the distance I'd travelled. Benji was first up and was asked to locate a certain bend in the river. We, on the other hand, were not told where we were going. Instead we had to follow Benji blindly, and when he stopped, we had to know where we were on the map. Easy peasy.

Despite my fear of night navigation, I soon felt a sense of calm as I journeyed with my fellow trainees and instructor. Perhaps it was a false sense of security, but I definitely felt a certain safety in numbers. Having five head torches all shining in the same direction also helped immensely. Our beams lit up the river bends, allowing us to count them as we travelled, meaning I could see which one we were on when Benji ground to a halt. Mission complete.

I was up next.

'I want you to bring us here,' our instructor said, pointing at my map to a contour line, a random bump in the ground. It was the sort of feature you'd struggle to find in broad daylight. My hand shook as I pulled off my glove to put my compass to work.

'Three hundred and fifty metres away,' I said under my breath, 'which will take us …which will take us…' My brain froze. It couldn't make the calculation. It was too busy freaking out. I took a deep breath and decided to shelve the time estimation and find the bearing instead. I eventually swivelled my body round to face where I needed to go, and then went back to tackle the question of how long it would take us. 'Around five minutes,'

I finally said. I looked around at my group, who were starting to look really cold and bored. 'This way,' I said pretending I knew what I was doing, before adding cheerily, 'Follow me.'

Those five minutes, those three hundred and fifty metres were probably the longest I've endured in my life. When the time had ticked through and the paces had added up, I came to an abrupt stop. 'We're here,' I shouted, trying to sound triumphant. After a quick scout to check the contour lines matched up, I was amazed that I could confidently state to the group that I had indeed found my mark. Maybe night navigation wasn't as bad as my mountain-running friends had made out.

It was only when I had ceased walking that I noticed my legs were shaking. I don't know whether it was from nerves that I wouldn't find the feature, whether it was from the mid-winter wind that whipped wildly around us, or from the sheer excitement that I had actually managed to nail it. My legs were obviously trying to tell me something.

We continued on through the night, taking turns to find different features. The time ticked well past midnight as we found Blue Lough. I hadn't even realised five hours had passed, so engrossed in the exercise had I become. It was such an eye-opener. I was starting to realise that with the right techniques, you could actually find your way in the pitch dark. It was also amazing to see that, with the right clothing and safety equipment, we could comfortably spend time in the mountains in the middle of January. Granted, I wouldn't have wanted to undertake such an exercise on my own. Having others there meant that if you twisted your ankle or swung off your bearing, someone was right there beside you to rescue you.

Maybe mountain runners with their aversion to darkness, to slowing down and to travelling in packs were missing out on something.

When we returned to our tents at 1 am, I was thrilled to see mine still in place. We bundled into them all, but I was still so buzzing from our night-time wander, that I could barely sleep. My head was still counting imaginary paces and wanting to check my compass and watch. My insomnia proved beneficial. At 3 am, my tent pegs gave way to the storm's strain and my tent duly took off, with me inside it.

'Help, help!' I screamed, as I sat bolt upright, the tent billowing wildly around my head. I was wise enough to know that if I got out of the tent at that point it would also blow away into the night.

Within a few seconds of my manic calls, I heard our instructor scrambling around outside. Soon the tent fabric started to straighten around me, followed by the words, 'that should do you for the night.'

I was mortified when I got up the next morning. My pride at nailing night navigation was erased by the fact I had had to be rescued once back at camp.

'Have you any idea where I found your pegs?' my instructor said, pointing dangerously close to a nearby river bend, a couple of metres away from where I had pitched. I hadn't even packed spare ones, not realising that tent pegs could be so dramatically lost and come so close to getting washed away. I had still a lot to learn.

With so much going on, I hadn't had much time to think about death or grief that weekend. I hadn't even noticed the absence of those thoughts. It wasn't until we sat down for our final briefing, before hiking out that morning, that I was brought back to the day of Pete's disappearance with a rude shock.

We were given a quick briefing at the campsite about search and rescue techniques for when someone goes missing in the mountains. I am certain this is the standard talk given on every expedition weekend, nothing aimed at me. I sat there listening to the ins and outs of how mountain rescue works. But instead of taking the lesson in, a horrible numbness crept through me. All I could think was, is that what they did when Pete went missing? Is this how they looked for him?

It also showed just how easily I could be caught off guard with something related to Pete's death. It could be something said, something I'd see, or something I'd touch that would directly bring me back to that day. It was just one of those things that I had to accept, knowing that there was no way I could anticipate being dragged kicking and screaming back to those memories.

We hiked out of the Annalong Valley, up towards the Brandy Pad and home via the Trassey's Track. The weather was dry but windy, so windy that, even on the low-lying, sheltered col between Slieve Beg and Slieve Commedagh, I was nearly blown off my feet. Strong gusts meant I had to at times hunker down to stop myself from toppling over.

Our instructors had purposely kept us off mountaintops and stuck to the valleys, knowing the accelerated wind speeds at higher levels could push someone over and cause a major injury. As we arrived back to base, we were informed that others had not been so fortunate. The very same day that we hiked out, two people died in the Mournes from the adverse weather conditions. It was a stark reminder of how just dangerous and unpredictable the mountains could be.

CHAPTER 12

FRAGILE

I was relieved to have completed my mountain-leader training. It meant I could go away now and practise what I'd learned, with the intention of signing up for the assessment before the end of the year. This part of my life, my plan to continue to get out in the mountains and qualify to bring others along, was going fine.

The rest of my life was not doing as well. After surfing the waves of sympathy and support during the initial weeks, I began to feel the sensation of cold water beneath me, lapping at my feet. I had been in a state of shock since Pete's death, wrapped in a numbness that protected me from any overwhelming thoughts and feelings. This surfing, however, could not last forever. Soon I found myself landing back to the shores of life in a series of bewildering crashes.

I hadn't been sure if my youngest son Cahal had really captured the reality of Pete's death, especially as he didn't appear to be listening that closely when I had told him and his brother. It was only when I didn't let Cahal have a biscuit one day that I realised Cahal was well aware of what was happening.

'I want Daddy,' he screamed, as I told him the biscuits were off limits. 'I want Daddy-horsey!'

My head went into meltdown. Did Cahal really want his daddy? Or did he just want someone to play horsey with? Or was this about me denying him a biccy? Did Pete used to give him biscuits on the sly and did Cahal want me to now do the same?

'But little one,' I replied, dropping down to his level and pulling him into an awkward hug. 'Daddy is gone.' His sobs continued on and on. Out of sympathy, perhaps to calm my own unease at the situation, I handed him the biscuit, at which his crying promptly stopped.

Cahal jumped out of my embrace and proceeded to trot happily away, my three-year-old genius having seemingly worked out which buttons to push. I vowed that was the last time I was going to let him use emotional blackmail, to use the tragedy of Pete's absence to get the treat he wanted.

Fortunately I was able to talk to Tim, one of Pete's friends, whose wife had unexpectedly passed away in her sleep a year before. Tim had young children who he was now raising as a single parent. He also had a year's worth of valuable experience that he was able and willing to share with me.

'I think the most useful thing I've learned over the past year,' Tim told me, 'is that kids take their emotional cues from you.' I wasn't sure if I had been showing any emotional cues in the past few weeks, given how numb I'd been at times feeling. 'Like, what I'm trying to say is that sometimes you've got to fake it to make it.' He told me how at times he had to project a slightly more positive image than how he was really feeling so that the kids felt happy and secure. Even then, his children sometimes worried that they too would drop down dead soon seeing how their own mother passed away without warning.

It was advice that seemed like another one of those fine-balancing acts that came with this terrain. I was to not pigeon-hole my emotions, but should feel free to talk about them. At the same time I had to take into account my children's emotions and keep check on my own deep dark feelings to make sure my offspring didn't adopt them as their own. It was a very fine line to walk.

'It seems like I'm lucky that my kids are so young,' I told Tim. 'They seem to be taking Pete's death as a simple fact, without really asking why it happened.' Even Cahal's occasional outbursts seemed to be less related to Pete and more a reaction to not getting what he wanted. 'I know these difficult questions about how or why Pete died will happen down the line, when they are a bit older, but at least I've the space right now to deal with other more pressing things.'

'I suppose it's about letting them talk about Pete whenever they want to,' Tim advised. 'Our family photos are still up around the house so they can still see pictures of their mum with us and we can talk about the good times.'

I had heard stories from people my own age, people who had had a parent die when they were young. Often compounding their loss was the fact that they were not allowed to talk about their mother or father afterwards. Their photos were taken down and their names no longer mentioned. This was confusing, often hurtful for them, not knowing whether or not they could talk about their deceased parent.

Just like the picture Aran drew that was placed with Pete in his coffin, Aran continued to draw his Daddy on our return home. I would always make an effort to sit down and listen so he could tell me what the picture was about. Typically it was a good memory of something Aran used to do with his Daddy, like going to the beach, eating ice-cream, reading books together or watching TV. Occasionally Aran would ask for the picture to be hung up on the wall, something I would always oblige.

I wasn't able to cope as well as Tim with keeping actual family portraits in place. Being reminded of the happier times captured in those stills only seemed to compound the loss I felt. I also felt a tinge of jealousy that in those photos Pete would never age. He would always remain through those photos the youthful face that never passed the age of fifty.

I was aware, however, that these photos could not be hidden away in case that action was misconstrued. So I hung family photos on the walls of the boys' bedrooms for them to look at whenever they felt the need. I put the rest of them in a corner of a sitting room that I only sometimes visited. The photos were there if any one of us felt the need to look at them, but they were not in a place where I would inadvertently stumble upon them.

As my head fog started to clear over the next few weeks, I started to see how bad my short-term memory had become. I realised I had developed a habit of repeating myself, of forgetting what I had told to whom, of just saying my latest concern over and over again to anyone who would listen. I must have bored my friends to tears. I became unable to hold any sort of proper conversation; unable to remember what people had told me about their own lives. Despite my social clumsiness, at least I had the permission to talk and share my thoughts and feelings rather than forever bottle them up.

With my short-term memory problems came other issues. Aran was meant to go to school one Monday morning and I went as usual to his room to help him with his school uniform. I knew I had placed some jogging bottoms in a drawer ready for him to wear. Only when I went to the drawer, they were gone.

'Did you already get your tracksuit bottoms?' I shouted out to him over my shoulder, assuming he had found them and put them on himself. I turned around to see Aran still in his pyjama bottoms looking confused by my question. There were of course other suitable tracksuit bottoms in the drawer, almost identical to the ones I was looking for. I became intent, however, on finding the ones I swore I had placed there.

My search soon turned into an obsession. I turned the house upside down looking for these sweat pants. 'If I'm not able to look after bits of school uniform,' I thought frantically, 'how am I ever going to look after myself or my kids?'

The escalation was way out of proportion, yet seemed logical in my head. If my husband could go for a run and not come home, then surely everything else would end up going catastrophically wrong as well.

Though Aran's tracksuit bottoms were eventually located (in the laundry room) having never made it as far as Aran's bedroom despite what my faulty memory told me, my reactions to everyday events continued to verge on crazy. Soon after this incident, Aran fell ill during the night. I was woken by his cries. It was the normal temperature and lethargy that children typically get when they've contracted a common bug. But when I saw the rash spread across his back, I totally freaked out.

I rushed Aran to the hospital, driving like a maniac through the dark.

'Please, please help me,' I begged the receptionist at the A&E desk, holding Aran in my arms. 'My son has meningitis.'

She took my details and made sure the triage nurse saw us quickly. I didn't want to mention the inevitability of death in front of my five-year-old, but I was sure that was the likely outcome.

'Now what seems to be the problem?' the triage nurse kindly asked us when we took a seat.

'His father passed away a few weeks ago,' I blurted out. 'I've already lost one. Please, I can't lose another.'

She looked at me sympathetically as she proceeded to calmly check Aran's vitals. She lifted up his pyjama top to check on his rash-like symptoms. I in turn wondered if she was going to check me over too. I had chest pains, I felt light-headed and was short of breath. I was most likely having a heart attack.

'I'm sorry to hear of your loss,' the nurse replied, addressing the diagnosis I'd first given her. 'I think Aran will be just fine. It looks like a viral infection, but we'll have the doctor check him out just in case.' On hearing these words, my heart attack symptoms mysteriously faded away.

I sat back in the waiting room with Aran after the consultation, collapsing into the plastic chair with relief. This feeling was soon replaced, however, with one that was profoundly mortified. Why had I over-reacted so much? Aran wasn't dying. He was merely suffering from a common childhood illness. I used to pride myself on being cool, calm and collected in difficult situations like these. Now I interpreted everything as having inevitably the worst ending. Was I slowly becoming paranoid in the way Pete did? Was I also going to come to a similar end?

I couldn't live anymore with this permanent abiding sense of doom. As soon as Aran was well, I followed up on the counselling services that I had lined up in case of emergency. A kind community-liaison woman from PIPS soon paid a house visit. She was part of this local service dedicated to the prevention of and support to those affected by suicide (Public Initiative for the Prevention of Suicide and Self Harm).

I made her a cup of tea, which she nursed gently as I spoke to her about what had happened. Acknowledging my thoughts and feelings and voicing them to someone else helped immensely. I didn't need to hide them anymore. She listened to them and confirmed that they were indeed normal, while challenging those that appeared harmful. Nothing was taboo in this safe setting. All of sudden I was able to examine and sort through them as they were set before me, to see what was worth keeping and what actually didn't make rational sense.

This process, which was followed up with every month, helped me stop fire fighting. It meant that, when I did meet a friend who had overcome depression, I was in a better place to listen and learn from them.

I had lost contact with most of my school friends over the years. Though I had briefly reconnected with one of them when I started my family, my move to Rostrevor meant that we had drifted apart again. It was only when I saw Finola standing there at Pete's funeral that the connection was quickly remade. I hadn't asked her to travel the six hours to the church, hadn't contacted her about Pete's illness or death. She had seen the death notice online and instinctively knew she should be there.

Up until then, I hadn't realised the significance of attending funerals within Ireland. I had wrongly thought it was just something for close friends and family, a moment where their privacy needed respect. After Pete's funeral, I came to understand that I had been mistaken. Even though I had lost touch with Finola, her presence at the funeral meant that I didn't need to explain to her all that had happened in the recent weeks. Not having to regurgitate it all was a relief. It meant that, when I was back in my hometown, I felt comfortable contacting her and meeting up with her again.

'I've been there,' she said, as we sat down at her kitchen table to catch up on the previous five years. We had thrown our two sets of kids into her sitting room, leaving them with Minecraft on the TV. There was no way we'd be disturbed for at least a few hours. 'I've had some really bad bouts of depression and, let's just say, it's not a pleasant experience.'

Pete had never really admitted to anyone, let alone to me, that he had depression. He blamed other things. It meant that he had never really vocalised to me what he was experiencing in terms of the disease, so I never fully understood what he was going through.

'It's like you feel so hopeless, so worthless, so joyless,' Finola explained. 'I remember looking at my kids and thinking, right now, I should feel love for them. But even though I knew what I should be feeling, I actually felt nothing, nothing at all. It was terrifying.'

Her words made my heart sink. When Pete told Aran and Cahal he loved them the night before died, did he know this was the right thing to say, even though he felt none of that love inside? Was he hoping that if he said these words, something would rekindle within him and save him from the inevitable in his mind?

'I've been told that depression is like being in a hole in a ground,' I replied, composing myself. 'You can be given a ladder, whether that's medication, counselling, but you ultimately have to climb out using the ladder. You still need to do some work yourself.'

'And that's exactly the problem,' Finola immediately cut in, 'you just don't have the energy to climb out of that hole. And to be honest, sometimes it's so dark down there, you don't even realise that you're in a hole, that you're supposed to try and climb out. You might think you're just in a really dark room, so you end up hitting off the walls searching for a door that doesn't even exist instead of climbing upwards. You might even need someone to break through from above and shine a light down.'

I remembered sitting with Pete one day after another of his counselling sessions. He had been given a booklet to take home with him about depression, one he had conveniently thrown to one side. I opened it up to see a checklist of symptoms. I sat Pete down and read them out to him one by one.

'Do you feel numb or upset?

Have you lost interest in things?

Do you feel alone in company?

Are you tired, have no energy, have sleep problems, feel worst in the mornings?

Have you had a change in weight or appetite?

Have you lost confidence in yourself?

Do you expect the worst and have negative thoughts?

Do you think that everything seems hopeless?

Do you hate yourself?

Do you have poor memory or concentration?

Do you put off things or not make decisions?

Can you be bothered to do everyday tasks?

Are you not doing things you used to enjoy?

Do you avoid seeing people?'

After a while, Pete stopped saying yes or even nodding his head. He just sat there. Even when I'd finished reaming them off, his face was expressionless.

'So does that mean I have depression?' he eventually said. It was such a terrifying list of symptoms, but at least reciting them had shone some sort of light down into his darkness.

'Well, according to this booklet, it appears so,' I replied. This moment of clarity proved, however, short-lived. Even after this discovery, I never heard Pete admitting to anyone that he was suffering from this condition.

'But *you* got out!' I said, reaching across the table to Finola. 'You're still here.' For whatever reason, Pete never found the ladder or the energy to make it back up. I was curious to find out how others like Finola had managed to somehow climb out.

'I suppose I got lucky,' Finola said after a while. 'I had really good support at the right time. I know not everyone gets or finds that.'

From the room next door, I could hear screams of excitement coming from our boys. They were probably busy pillaging some poor Minecraft village, without a care in the world.

'I know there's so much stigma around depression,' Finola continued, trying not to lose her train of thought. 'But if you've had it, the last thing you want to do is talk about it. Speaking about it only reminds you about how shit you felt. Like it's really hard dragging up all those memories.'

'It sounds a bit like having post-traumatic stress disorder,' I replied, offering some sort of explanation. 'Like remembering what it was like to be depressed just re-traumatises you, is that right?'

'I suppose,' Finola said, breaking eye contact to stare across the room.

'Oh, I'm so sorry…' I said, hoping to hastily backtrack. 'I didn't mean to upset you.'

'No, no. It's not that at all,' Finola said, swiftly coming back to me. 'I'm just trying to find the right words to describe to you what's its like. It's really fuckin' scary to go through depression. It's just…I don't want to frighten you.'

I appreciated Finola trying her best to help me understand what Pete had gone through. It helped me understand.

'I know now that I have to manage myself,' Finola said. 'If I start to feel myself slipping, I can recognise the signs. It doesn't always work, but thankfully I have a couple of tools to stop myself from sliding back down into the hole.'

Since Pete's death, some had asked me how to help people they know who are going through depression. I never knew what to say. Despite Pete following best practice, it didn't stop his demise. Speaking with Finola helped restore some hope that people can recover from depression.

'I'm thriving now,' she told me. 'I've a job, I've relationships, I can go out and do things. It seemed totally impossible when I was in it, but depression *can* go away. And if it does come back, I know I can also live with it.'

My conversation with Finola put another piece into the puzzle of understanding what had happened to Pete. I had also seen for myself how Finola had to summon up considerable courage to even tell me her story. Even if there is less and less stigma around mental health issues, it seemed exhausting for survivors if they chose to speak about them. Physically Finola looked worn out by the end of conversation, even though she had helped me no end.

It meant that, when I went home, I was able to finally look at the letters people had sent Aran and Cahal since their Dad had died. They had flooded in after the funeral, when I had asked Pete's friends and family to write down their memories of Pete so that his sons would be able to read them later in their life.

The letters spoke of how amazing Pete was, how he was so intelligent yet such a kind mentor. They spoke of Pete's achievements, which were indeed numerous and impressive. So many of the letters said how Pete was such a genuinely nice guy, someone who was easy to get on with and very likeable.

I always knew that Pete was popular, but it wasn't until I sat down and read these words that I realised how much he was valued and loved. What was scary though was that, after living with a depressed version of Pete, I had actually forgotten how incredible a person he was. Depression had caused him to become a shadow of the person he really was. Going through letter after letter, all I could think was, what a waste of a life, what a tragic loss. The last six months of his life were a total aberration. They just illustrated to me how much depression had distorted and beaten Pete down.

I had admittedly felt angry at times with Pete for his decision to end his life. I was annoyed that I had been left to clean up the mess. Having spoken with Finola, I understood a bit more how depression changes a person and can so radically pervert the way they think. I had heard it not from a carer, but from someone who had also been directly afflicted by the illness.

It meant that I knew that I could no longer be mad with Pete. His suicide wasn't his fault. Instead I had come to realise that all this time my anger had been misplaced. In fact, I was instead fucking furious at his disease, not him, and how it had destroyed Pete's life.

After reading all the letters, I put them away. Aran and Cahal were still too young to comprehend their meaning or to value their contents. That would come at a later stage. Instead I purchased a beautiful blanket box and placed the letters inside. Together with them I put everything I had found of Pete's that would help them eventually get to know their Dad.

I put Pete's tattered wallet in along with his well-used passport and various business cards. I placed in the box his CD collection of 80s music, with hits from Led Zepplin, U2, Van Morrison and The Police. At our wedding, I'd been given pictures of Pete from when he was a baby. The box seemed the appropriate place to keep them safe. I was always surprised how similar

Aran looked to baby Pete at the same age. A rugby ball, a haul of medals from various road races, his favourite running shirt also went in there. I couldn't help but add a Peppa Pig book that Pete used to read to the boys when they were small about Daddy Pig's haphazard antics.

It took a while before I allowed myself to put in Pete's medical records and an advice book about depression that he had received. There was a part of me that didn't know what to do with these papers. It didn't feel right to throw them out.

I reconciled myself to the fact that it needed to be a 'warts and all' box, a comprehensive treasure trove of items that really explained the ins and outs of who Pete was. I left a place for some of Pete's ashes when they were ready, a gap the right size to place two small urns, one each for Aran and Cahal, for them to have when older.

I placed the blanket box in the heart of our home so we could all come and go from it as we pleased. Sometimes the boys would delve in to it and take some of Pete's possessions out and play made-up games with them. I'd quietly dip in when alone to flick through the boys' letters. At other times Cahal would use the box's lid as a table. It was the perfect size and shape to build his Lego figures.

We were all doing whatever we could just to become a little less fragile.

CHAPTER 13

ORIENTEERING

I was constantly on the look out for things to do to help our family rebuild our life. Part of this was because I felt compelled to spend more time with my boys, to make sure I was there in case the loss of their father all became too much. To do this, I knew I had to also mind myself, to make sure I was physically and mentally well enough for whatever came down the road.

There was no map for how to journey through this period of time. All I could do was make educated guesses. If a strategy worked, that was well and good and was earmarked for repetition. If not, I quickly binned it.

The mountains had taught me such flexibility. If the weather out there turned bad, I'd put on more layers or descend the exposed mountainside. If the mist came in, I'd pay more attention to the map or change route to one more easily navigated. If I came across cliffs or dangerous ground, I'd quickly change direction. The unpredictability of the mountains and the myriad of issues they'd throw my way had taught me the importance of adapting come what may.

I had discovered years beforehand that orienteering was the perfect sport for our young family. When Pete was still with us, we used to attend local orienteering events. With orienteering being a niche sport in Northern

Ireland with relatively few participants, sometimes only twenty or thirty at events, we soon became regulars whose faces were recognised. The boys became notorious for stealing any post-race treats that were available at the finish line.

In my thirties, I used to go orienteering every week, choosing the longest and hardest courses of around eight kilometres, where the control flags were hidden in difficult-to-reach places deep in forests or on remote mountainsides. Now, in my forties and with my children in tow, I gravitated to the other end of the orienteering spectrum. We would enter the easiest courses on offer; the two-kilometre jaunts on prominent paths where the flags were placed in obvious places. You'd practically fall over the flags while seeing them from a mile away. And there was no more running, not even the briefest of jogs. When I was out with Aran and Cahal, the course was all done at a leisurely walk, with mandatory stops on route to pick up sticks, smell flowers and throw random stones into adjacent fast-flowing rivers.

Even though they were young, Aran and Cahal loved orienteering. They enjoyed getting their hands on the map, studying it intensely, pretending they could read it just like the grown-ups. They begged to have the electronic dibbers wrapped tight around their fingers, barely able to contain their excitement at the idea of making the flag's box beep when they successfully found it. Having nine or ten control flags that they had to find on route meant that the two-kilometre course was broken down perfectly into bits. It made it less of a death march, a seemingly never-ending hour-long walk. Instead the boys regarded orienteering as a type of treasure hunt to find red and white flags hidden in a yet to be discovered land, their ultimate prize a piece of paper with their random split times at the finish.

It wasn't just our children who were kept busy while orienteering. We all had our roles to play. I was the chief map reader, there as back up when Aran and Cahal led us astray. Pete was head dog handler, with Tom also accompanying us on the walks. My only stipulation was, if Tom was coming, he was not allowed to pee on the posts that held up the orienteering flags. I didn't want to have the orienteering organisers having to deal with dog wee when collecting them up.

With Pete now gone, I found myself gravitating back to the sport. I was in no position to enter the hardest courses, having lost my appetite for hard training and racing. It just seemed like a good excuse to get out again with my family, to get some exercise in as well as a chance to spend some quality time together.

In early February, I saw both the Northern Ireland Score Championships and Night Orienteering Championships were on the same day. It was a mere six weeks after Pete's death, still early days. Yet I figured it was still worth going. I reasoned that if I found the excursion too much, I could easily shortcut and head home, and erase orienteering from my trial and error recovery plan.

I felt slightly nauseous as I lined up with others in Seskinore Forest outside Omagh to register for the day's first event, the Score Championships. It felt like a re-run of when I stood outside Cahal's playgroup and fretted about who knew, who didn't know, whether I should say something first? This time, it was very obvious that Pete wasn't there. He would have always turned up with me to such events and made small talk as I sorted out the entries. His absence was stark and clear.

Just like when I saw my school friend Finola after all those years, it was the people who had attended Pete's funeral who made the first advance. There was no need for a recap, only a quick catch-up. 'How are you guys doing?' they all asked.

I took a deep breath before answering each time. 'Yeah,' I said. 'We're doing okay, thanks for asking.' I felt relieved as I said it, because it was actually the truth. We were doing not too bad, all things considered.

A few more orienteers came up afterwards and offered their condolences. They were mainly the older orienteers, people who had already experienced grief in other guises in their own lives. I knew it was not easy for them, but I so appreciated their kind words. It made me feel better about being there.

Orienteers are usually sent off individually after minute or so intervals, to stop them following each other. With it being a score event, where you're free to choose which direction you head in, this time we had a mass start. This is why there were sixty orienteers huddled round the race organiser at the edge of the forest around midday, waiting to hear the final instructions. People jumped up and down nervously as they readied themselves to compete for Championship titles. They also wanted to keep warm, eager to run into the sheltered forest, as the mid-February rain threatened to break overhead.

It was a nice, small group of people to be with, many of whom I knew. I felt comfortable in their midst. Aran and Cahal were the youngest participants there. They were also the shortest; I made them stand close to me to make sure they weren't stood on by an adult orienteer limbering up. Many of the orienteers bent down to wish them well with their race. Dogs barked excitedly, waiting for the off. Our own dog, Tom, played it cool. He had done such events before. I was glad that he wasn't that excitable.

Out of everyone, I was probably the most nervous one that day. I had to map read as well as act as chief dog-handler, taking over Pete's role for the first time.

With a swift countdown from ten to one, the orienteers were soon unleashed. They scattered in all manner of directions, Aran and Cahal unsure of which way to head. 'Let's go and pick up this control,' I said, pointing to their maps, before marching off confidently along a path to find the flag, hoping they would follow me.

With a score event, orienteers have to choose which controls to get and in which order. They also have to do so within an allocated time period. Our event that day gave us forty-five minutes to rake up as many points as we could. If we arrived at the finish after three-quarters of an hour had passed, punitive penalties were applied.

In addition to map reading and time keeping, I also had the tasks of herding Aran and Cahal in the right direction.

'Mind the puddle,' I'd shout as I saw Aran and Cahal rushing off to see who could do the biggest splash. 'There's the flag,' I'd say, pointing in the opposite direction they'd just run off in, trying to get them back on track. 'Go beep it!'

If the control flag was positioned on slightly rougher ground, I'd have to lift each child up by the armpits so that they could reach the box without tripping over some tree root or embedded stone. If I'd inadvertently let Aran put his dibber into the box before his younger brother, I'd then have to act as head mediator. Cahal would have a minor meltdown in the middle of the forest when he realised his sibling had beaten him to the flag. 'It's okay,' I'd whispered calmly to Cahal in his ear. 'You can be first to find the next one.' His tears would quickly dry up if he saw another child running off to find a flag. All of a sudden, his competitive self would click in; even at the tender age of three, he was damned if he was going to let that other kid beat him. This competitive streak he had obviously inherited from Pete.

Throughout all this mayhem, I also had to make sure Tom had a sufficient walk. I couldn't just get a flag or two and call it a day after five minutes. I had to keep orienteering for the full forty-five minutes to make sure our dog didn't feel short-changed.

It was all so perfectly distracting. In fact, it seemed like an ideal way to spend time as part of our grieving process.

We eventually arrived at the finish with barely two minutes to spare. With total scores of one hundred and forty each, Cahal and Aran took second and third in the Northern Ireland Score Championships within the under-ten age group, their positions only separated by who got to the finishing box first. Their reward was a bag of mini chocolate Easter eggs each. There was not a bit of shyness at the official prize-giving as they rushed up and collected these prizes with glee. For the first time in a long time, I smiled. It was only as I felt it stretch across my face that I realised I hadn't smiled in a very long time.

Bringing the boys on the night orienteering course that evening was a long shot. I knew they'd be tired from their score event; that orienteering twice in one day was a bit much. I really wanted, however, to go out on the course and have a bit of night navigation practice myself, to put it towards my mountain-leader preparation.

One of the profoundest changes I faced when Pete died was not having a second parent to hand. If I wanted to go out on a run, I couldn't just signal to Pete I'd be back in an hour and happily jog out the door. The boys were too big for a running buggy, yet still too small to be left alone in the house. It meant that I always had to have some sort of childcare lined up if I wanted to do anything without them.

With Pete's death, competitive racing had also become a distant memory.

When Pete was alive, I would often travel to faraway places on Ireland's coast like Dingle, Donegal, or Achill to compete in championship events, often spending two nights away from home. Such adventures were no longer possible with two small kids constantly in tow.

Fortunately, the orienteering community came to my aid that night, something they would do time and time again as the weeks and months passed.

'Do you want me to babysit Aran and Cahal so that you get a run out?' Juls had emailed me before the day. She was officially the orienteering sporting clubs coordinator, but she also was a brand-new mum who loved kids. She knew exactly what a break meant for me.

'Would you?' I replied. I didn't want to impose or stop her from entering the event. Then I remembered what Henry said. Say yes to everything.

Juls came to the event centre exceptionally well prepared. She had building blocks, markers and reading books to distract them while I was away. She hadn't expected my kids would be high on sugar from the mini eggs they had won earlier that day. I decided to not tell her that additional bit of information in case she withdrew her offer.

'Go!' Juls shouted at me as I loitered around my kids. 'Go for your run, will ye?' practically escorting me out the door.

I felt a bit nervous heading out into the forest at night with only a dim head-torch to light up my way. Unlike my mountain-leader training, I'd be on my own in there, without the comfort of a group effort. There was no mass start this time, people being set off on one-minute intervals instead. Forests can also appear ten times darker than the mountains, what with the branches blocking out any moonlight, and likewise ten times creepier.

Needless to say, I got lost within seconds in some horrible undergrowth.

I had forgotten to count my paces and had probably overshot the mark. Not knowing how far I had gone, I had to double-back and re-find the path I'd originally been on. Cursing myself, I watched as a head torch sped past me to my left before disappearing into the foliage. At least someone else was out there that night. At least I had some sort of company.

'Concentrate!' I whispered to myself. 'It doesn't matter how fast you go. Just practise your night nav.' My laboured breathing was creating a fog before my eyes. I held my breath long enough for the mist to clear so I could take a proper look at my map. It didn't help that I wasn't as fit as I'd normally be. I had forgotten that fact. 'It's not a race,' I reminded myself. 'Just find the flags, nice and slow.'

Slowing down was what I needed to do to properly navigate. As I found the first control, then the next, then the next, I started to enjoy myself. All my mind could focus on was the next control I was looking for and the direction I needed to go in after that. Anything beyond that was superfluous. Even when I made a mess of control number nine, I realised I didn't care. Out there in the night, no one knew how well or how badly I was doing; no one could see how fast or slow I was going. There was no pressure, no expectations, no stress.

Doing an hour's worth of orienteering was the surprising formula that helped me both physically and mentally that day. Even when I got to the end, the marshal manning the finish gave me a big hug and told me, 'it was good to see me out.'

I sprinted back to the centre when I eventually remembered I'd abandoned my kids with Juls. I burst into the hall to see the mayhem Aran and Cahal had caused while I was gone. The building blocks had been launched to the far corners of the room. Cahal was busy scribbling over the reading books Juls had brought along. Juls was sitting in the midst of it all. 'We've had such great craic,' she exclaimed. She looked totally exhausted yet perfectly content. I still felt guilty about leaving my boys with other people. I always thought they were doing it out of sympathy and that they hated every minute of it. Seeing Juls on her hands and knees playing with the boys, I realised that maybe some people actually don't mind babysitting. It had never crossed my mind that some may actually choose childminding over orienteering.

Coming back to my children after stumbling around a darkened forest for an hour, looking for random circles on a map had somehow done me the world of good. I'm not sure if it was the fact I had gone for a run or had a chance to orienteer. Maybe it was because I had hung out with some friendly familiar faces. Or perhaps it was just because I had had a brief break from being a single mum. All I knew was that, if something helped me feel okay for an instant, then I should just go with it.

CHAPTER 14

QUEENS OF THE QMDS

As part of my Mountain Leader award, I needed to do at least forty Quality Mountain Days or QMDs for my logbook. Though I had already spent way more than forty days out on the mountains during my decade of mountain running, days that I deemed to be 'quality', I had always been doing the same sort of thing. My time was typically spent running from one peak to another and another, and that was basically it. Now I needed to get out and do a broader range of mountain-based tasks, to cover all the gaps that the Award's extensive syllabus demanded.

During the training weekend, one of the instructors had a look at my logbook that I had managed to rustle up from my mountain-running past. The main areas I needed to work on were steep ground, emergency rope work and group management. Unfortunately these were areas I could not go out and practise alone. I needed a person to tie my rope to so I could practise pulling them up and down. I had to have some sort of human, or ideally a couple of them, to practise group management while out on the mountains, to ensure I kept them safe and sound. The only problem was that I didn't know where to source some guinea pigs that were willing to let me practise on them.

I was of course not alone in needing a buddy on the hills. As chance would have it, at an orienteering event, I bumped into another trainee mountain leader with the same quandary as me. Rachy had heard on the outdoor grapevine that I needed to rack up some QMDs, and she was wondering if she could tag along with me.

Rachy wasn't the type of person I'd normally hang out with. Long story short, she didn't look like a mountain runner. She had various piercings on her ears and through her nose, cropped hair and looked like she could go ten rounds with Mike Tyson. Yet when she spoke, she had the most gentle, friendly voice that seemed at odds with her muscular self.

'I hear you're into mountain running,' Rachy said as way of introduction. 'I'd love to get more into the sport.' I could feel my eyebrows rise up as far as my hairline. I'd heard people before say that they'd like to mountain run, but would never bother their arse to go and try. I suspected Rachy was another one of those 'all talk, no action' sorta gals.

I was soon to discover that I was wrong. When Rachy said she was going to try something, she genuinely meant it. When we met, she was training to be not just a mountain leader like me, but a fully-fledged outdoor instructor. Soon enough she rattled off every outdoor sport that she already was handy at. Kayaking, mountain biking and rock climbing were the top three outdoor activities that I had abandoned earlier in my life for being too cold and dangerous. Nothing could seemingly put Rachy off. If it was outdoors and involved action, Rachy was up for it.

We agreed to meet on the slopes of Butter Mountain, just below the Mourne Mountains' Spelga Dam. It was an area known for its grassy slopes as opposed to scary cliffs, but the close together contour lines on the map showed that the area was steep enough to practise what we needed. I had already experienced its gradient in my previous life as a mountain runner.

I had to descend this section during a race, but my grips couldn't hold me upright no matter how much I dug in. I ended up sliding my way down on my bum, having to steer my Lycra-clad rear end carefully so to not shave any ass skin off on the granite boulders that were strewn across the slope.

Butter Mountain was also an area that had a conveniently positioned car park right at its base. This meant that Rachy and I didn't have to do an hour-long walk just to get into a suitable place to do rope work. Even if we wanted the exercise, I didn't have the time for such a hike; I had a total of three hours free before I had to collect my kids. Time was of the essence.

'Where do you want to head?' I asked, as Rachy and I stared up at the mountainside. We both scanned the incline, eventually agreeing on a rocky outcrop just above us as the perfect place to start. We threw on our rucksacks and started to walk towards it.

'So when are you hoping to do your assessment?' I asked Rachy, breaking the silence as we started to climb.

'Maybe this coming Easter,' she replied. 'I've already done about ninety QMDs, so I'm just looking to brush up at this stage.' I had also wanted to do my assessment that coming Easter, but had been told it was too soon. It was barely two months away and my instructors had told me to take my time and prepare for an autumn sit. I also had nowhere near Rachy's ninety days, which was apparently a good number if you wanted to pass first time. Word was that forty QMDs were an absolute bare minimum pre-requisite.

'Well if you're that close to doing the exam, why don't you set up first?' I said when we got to the top of the rock. 'I'll be your client, and you can rope me up and guide me down this drop.'

'Sure,' Rachy replied, as she dumped her bag at our site and proceeded to whip out her rope. I was kind of glad Rachy agreed to take the lead. I wanted to see how she tied her anchors, how she positioned herself near the edge, how she set up her belay so that if I fell she'd catch me.

'Now Moire, I want you to sit yourself down right over there,' Rachy said calmly, immediately snapping into mountain-leader mode. 'If you're cold, maybe throw on an extra layer. Also, it's a good time to have a snack if you're feeling peckish at all.' I'd just had my breakfast, so politely declined, knowing though this was all role-play. I nodded obediently and made myself comfortable while Rachy continued with her spiel. 'Now we just need to get ourselves down this small step safely, so I'm going to use this rope to help you walk down.'

Step? I thought. I looked at the big rock that Rachy was preparing to lower me off. That was definitely not a 'step'. And there was no walking down that thing either. Rachy's interpretation of what was going on needed a reality check.

'I'm going to be climbing down a massive boulder, Rachy,' I said, not wanting to mention the obvious. 'Not walking down a blummin' set of stairs!'

'Ah now,' she replied. 'I don't want to be freaking you out, do I? Look it, I wouldn't be taking out this rope unless we were having a proper full-blown emergency, so my role is to make sure you keep nice and calm.'

'But you're lying to me,' I said, not sure if I wanted to role-play anymore.

Rachy in turn looked me straight in the eye.

'You'll be totally fine,' she replied, refusing to flinch. 'I promise that I'll get you down safely and we'll be home soon. Trust me.'

I half expected her to tell me to sit down and shut up at this stage, but instead she calmly went back to her rope to make a loop that would fit around my waist. Rachy was a model of serenity. If the wind was howling and the mist was down, she'd be the kinda person you'd want as your guide.

I had been told that the Mountain Leader award wasn't just about mountain skills. If anything, the main emphasis was on leadership. The mountains can throw anything and everything at you in terms of weather and terrain. Being out there meant you were challenged both mentally and physically. Could you be trusted to take other people out into such an unpredictable environment? If anything happened, would you be able to lead them out of danger without losing your own head?

I could see that Rachy's training as an outdoor instructor was coming to the fore. It wasn't just about knowing what to do, which I had been solely focused on, but how you did it as well.

'I know you're well able to get down this last bit,' she continued on as she found a suitable anchor to hold the rope fast, 'so if you listen carefully to my instructions, we'll be out of here soon.' Even though I knew this was all made up, I found her encouragement heartening. Rachy continued on with some light banter to distract me, her pretend client, from the emergency rope-work procedure that lay ahead. Then, when she was finally ready, she briefed me succinctly so I knew exactly what to expect. She made sure I understood everything, that every question I had was answered, before finally letting me descend. And as I lowered myself off the boulder, she guided me down with clear instructions all the way.

'That was really good,' I said, once I hit sold ground below. 'Like, I felt I was in really safe hands.'

'Thanks,' Rachy replied. 'I wasn't sure if my rope wasn't going to be long enough to get you down, but it looks like it did the job.'

'Now you tell me!' I said, realising she had fooled me with her composure. Just like Tim had suggested I'd have to emotionally 'fake it to make it' sometimes with my own kids, here was Rachy faking it out in the mountain so that I remained calm while dangling off her rope. It seemed like I was learning things while mourning that I could use to become a better mountain leader, and equally some tricks I was learning out on the mountains that could help me on my grief journey. The synergies were not lost on me.

I clambered back up the boulder to take my turn with the rope. As I waited for Rachy to untie her knots, I couldn't help but ask her why she'd decided to become an outdoor instructor.

'You know, I had a good job running my own web and graphic design business in Bangor,' Rachy replied. 'But then one day, less than two years ago, I was out riding my bike, coming back from a spin with three friends. I was just about to turn off for home when a driver came out of nowhere, ploughed into our group at seventy miles an hour. One of the guys, Gavin, was thrown eighty metres away and died later that day from internal injuries. Another broke his back and ribs. The third had to take time off work afterwards, he was so psychologically scarred.'

'Shit Rachy, that's horrible.'

'Yeah, I know,' she said. 'And what makes it worse is that I walked away from it all without a scratch. Like I did what I could, I held Gavin's hand and begged him to hold on, told him it wasn't his time. But it wasn't enough. Emotionally, of course, I was a mess. I felt so guilty that it wasn't me who was hurt or worse.' I didn't know what to say. 'It just made me think,' Rachy continued, 'if your life can change as quick as that, then you better get on with living it. So I quit my job, which I wasn't happy with anyway, and started to retrain as an outdoor instructor. It was always something I had wanted to do, so I just got on with doing it.'

For having been through such a traumatic accident, it was amazing

Rachy had emerged from it relatively unscathed. Weeks later she shared with me the trauma of having to testify against the man who had driven into them, of writing down a detailed statement of how it had destroyed their lives. She spoke of the devastating effect her friend's death had on her and the survivor's guilt that still remained. She told me of the heart-breaking reality of her cycling mate who, despite rehab and several hopeful signs of recovery, still couldn't walk. Whoever thought life was meant to be fair just didn't read the instruction book.

'Most outdoor instructor trainees are in their twenties, while I'm thirty-five,' Rachy said, handing me the rope so I could set up. 'But I'm kinda glad I'm a bit older, as it means that I know what I want and I'm prepared to work hard to get it. Loads of people have said I'm really brave for taking this risk, that I'm living the dream. But at the time I just felt in my gut I wasn't happy where I was. Even before the accident, I hadn't been excited about anything for ages.' It seemed like embarking on such a radical life change was less terrifying for Rachy than not daring to take the risk in the first place.

Somehow from that carnage Rachy had learned that life was too short for regrets. At the age of forty-three, with a bit of luck, I was barely halfway through life. Was I going to be a gravestone with words etched on me to remember what had been? Or was I going to be a sign with an arrow pointing towards potential new realities?

Her *carpe diem* attitude meant that, once we were done our three-hour session, Rachy announced she was heading off to do a bit of rock climbing on Hen Mountain straight after with some mates.

'Isn't it getting a bit windy to be out climbing on exposed rock?' I asked. I was quite looking forward to heading home to have a quiet cup of tea before spending the afternoon with the kids in the park.

'Yeah, the weather's getting a wee bit spicy alright,' Rachy replied. 'But sure we'll wrap up and be grand.'

I was slowly learning that Rachy's version of 'spicy' weather was my version of 'feckin' freezing.' I secretly hoped Rachy's optimism wasn't infectious. I quite liked being cynical.

A few weeks later Rachy and I met up again, this time to take on Slieve Roosley. It's a minor hill north of Rostrevor village, one that walkers rarely frequent. Its lack of popularity stems from the fact that it's a bog-infested, heather-ridden place covered in ankle-breaking boulders with no paths to speak of. It was perfect for us now self-christened Queens of the QMDs to practise our navigation on.

Rachy was ridiculously cheery when she pulled up in her car.

'I'm so looking forward to this,' she said, hauling her rucksack out of her boot.

'Are you serious?' I replied. Looking up at the sky, I could see rain threatening. Mist was surely on its way. If there ever was a reason to be 'bah, humbug' about mountain walking, it was right then.

'I've always wanted to check out Slieve Roosley,' Rachy said as we crossed the barbed wire fence on to the mountainside. 'I heard it's a great place for nav practice.' Just as she said it, her boots sunk deep into a wet and cold marsh that she'd failed to see in front of us, water spilling over their tops. 'Oops,' was all she said as she continued to plod on over to the marsh's other side. Even the prospect of spending the morning with soggy feet couldn't put Rachy off.

The terrain continued to be wet underfoot, making walking through it laborious. With our heads down, Rachy somehow managed to find another reason to be happy.

'Ohhh, look at this,' she exclaimed, bending over some undergrowth. She was checking out some lurid lime-coloured plant that I'd probably run over a million times without a second thought.

'Sphagnum moss,' Rachy declared. 'It can hold up to twenty times its own weight in water. When it's really wet, it changes into this bright green colour.'

'It's wet?' I said. 'No shit.' Brushing off my sarcasm, Rachy swiftly continued on with her botanic lesson.

'It's also acidic, so stops bacteria and fungi from growing,' she said. 'And because it's so absorbent as well, they used it in World War I as a wound dressing. Interesting fact, no?' I begrudgingly admitted to Rachy that it was maybe, perhaps, sort of interesting.

The deeper issue I was battling with was that mountain flora and fauna was another item on the list of things I needed to know for the assessment. I was experiencing that overwhelmed feeling again. I had already tried to sit down at home and swot up on the subject, but had miserably failed to retain anything. It was probably a hangover from the days when someone tried to teach me the Latin names of plants, which only served to put me off the subject forever.

When I went home after our session, I looked sphagnum moss up in a textbook. Somehow the academic description made a little more sense once I had seen it in real life. I suppose that's why the Award insists on people getting out and recording quality mountain days. There was no way I was going to be able to learn how to be a mountain leader by sitting at home and reading theoretical books. I'd have to get out there, particularly with others, to learn, practise and experience all the facets of mountain life.

On a few more outings on my own, I started to see how a bit of flora and fauna knowledge could even help me with my mountain-running speed. I discovered the beautiful yet delicate bog asphodel sprouting on large sections around Pigeon Rock Mountain during the warm summer months. Their bright yellow flowers standing erect on their stalks could be easily seen from afar. Getting closer to them, I finally understood the origins of its name. It loved flowering profusely in wet, shoe-sucking ground. Running around instead of through bog asphodel not only stopped me from destroying this pretty mountainside sight. It also allowed me to run faster on drier ground as opposed to wading through sticky bog. Thanks to my mountain-leader training, I was able to add 'navigation by foliage' as a mountain-running skill to my repertoire.

Rachy and I continued to meet up most weeks. One thing I couldn't perfect on those sessions, however, was my group management skills. To do that, I needed to find people who would allow me to lead them in the mountains. Fortunately I had already worked out exactly where I would find such ready and willing volunteers.

CHAPTER 15

HAPPY OUT ADVENTURES

My idea to set up a mountain-running venture was still very much in my mind. I had already been involved in the sport for well over a decade. During that time I had raced all around Ireland, winning the Irish Mountain Running Championships twice in my younger days. Mountain running was my passion.

I wasn't sure, however, whether I could start it without first securing my Mountain Leader award. I had already completed the training and done sixteen hours of first aid rescue emergency care. In addition, I had managed to attend a Leadership in Fell Running Fitness session via Athletics Northern Ireland. I just didn't know if these certificates were sufficient to start taking clients on.

To find out what I needed qualification-wise, I spoke with other outdoor instructors, many within senior management posts. They advised me that, though qualifications were indeed important, experience was paramount. The clincher was ultimately whether or not I could get insurance to start my outdoor activities. After many stressful Internet searches and detailed phone calls, I found a company that was happy to insure me for the mountain-running training and guiding activities that I wanted to do. It was all systems go after that.

Once I knew my company could function, I had to give it a name. I wanted something suitably generic so I could branch out into whatever activity proved most popular as time went on. I also didn't want to give it a name that was purely related to mountain running. If men, women, or children wanted to walk, run, ski, cycle, glide, skate, even stand in the outdoors with me, then I wanted an entity that told them they could do exactly that. I finally wanted a name with a nod to my Irish origins. 'Happy out' is what the Irish say when they're dead chuffed with their situation. Seeing that I'm always happiest when outdoors, 'Happy Out Adventures' felt a suitable name to work under.

Years of running in mountain races had already shown me something that needed teaching. I felt compelled to put on a basic navigation course specifically designed for mountain runners.

I started mountain running back in 2006, competing at first in the Wednesday night Leinster League series organised by the Irish Mountain Running Association, or IMRA as it's known for short. These mid-week races took place on pre-marked courses throughout the Dublin and Wicklow Mountains. Even if some of the courses went off-trail, someone had always gone out beforehand and placed red and white tape on the route to make sure everyone knew which way to go.

The races IMRA held on weekends were a different kettle of fish. Not only were they often longer and scaled taller, more remote mountains; the vast majority of them had no markings to speak of. It was up to the mountain runners to navigate their way to a series of points within the mountain range and back. Marshalls or pre-placed orienteering punches were used to testify whether you had reached those spots or not. Such races weren't therefore just about speed. They also tested your ability to navigate. This additional requirement caused the number of participants to drop sharply off. Not many wanted to have their sense of direction tested as well as their ability to mountain run. It was all a bit too much.

To me, those unmarked races looked so much more daring, exciting, challenging than the sedate mid-week ones. I so badly wanted to compete in those weekend races that I did everything I could to learn how to use a map and compass. I inevitably made my fair share of mistakes while figuring out my north from south, getting lost in a bewildering array of ways, but it was well worth it just so I could take part.

Soon enough, after I turned up to enough of these races, people at various finish lines began to confide in me navigation horror stories, runners getting ridiculously lost while out on mountain courses. When I probed deeper, I found many of those runners who had gone astray shared a remarkably similar navigation strategy. They typically went out there with the intention of following the runner in front of them, no matter who they were.

This follow-my-leader strategy was particularly popular if the person in front was male and was sporting a mountain-running club singlet. It didn't matter in the slightest if that man who had paid his club fees hadn't a clue where he were going, or if he was just following an equally lost runner in front of him. A vision of a bunch of lemmings on the mountainside came quickly to mind.

This was despite the fact that all of these runners religiously carried maps and compasses with them as part of the required mandatory gear. I soon discovered that few of them actually knew how to use these instruments if they were all of a sudden lost. Some seasoned mountain runners still had their maps and compasses in their original shop-bought packaging after many years of racing. Event organisers typically assumed everyone had this skill as they allowed them to line up in a race. If you didn't, on your own head be it.

In the Mourne Mountains, this lack of navigation skills was annually demonstrated on races that climbed Slieve Commedagh, a popular mountain near the coast used on several un-marked weekend races. If the finish lay in the seaside town of Newcastle, the quickest and easiest route off Slieve Commedagh was to head north off the summit for about six hundred metres, and then in a north-east direction until you hit the forest.

When the gods wanted to watch the mountain-running community pit themselves against each other and allowed visibility to be good, it was a simple and fun descent of twenty to thirty minutes over heathery bog and then down through Donard forest. But if the gods weren't interested in how the race panned out and let the mist came down, those racers who came unprepared were ultimately doomed, destined to not see Newcastle again for at least another hour. Getting lost on Slieve Commedagh's slopes, with only sheep as company, was not for the faint-hearted. What made things worse was that Slieve Commedagh's summit cairn was lined to the east and west by steep, scary cliffs. My gut said it was only a matter time before a runner mistakenly took a wrong turn and catapulted themselves down a set of them.

Another aspect that made the running of navigation training courses so timely was a recent rule change by the Fell Running Association or FRA, the UK's mountain-running governing body, regarding GPS device usage during races. GPS had crept into mountain-running circles over the years. It was totally understandable. If suitably charged and the wearer knew how to operate it, they were brilliant at ensuring you knew exactly where you were. It meant you didn't have to learn to use a map and compass. With a press of a button, you could have a self-correcting arrow on your wrist telling you to go 'that-a-way.' The only problem was, in a race scenario, they gave you a distinct advantage over someone navigating manually. Map and compass were slightly slower to use and were occasionally prone to operator failure.

People continued to turn up to races with their navigation instruments of preference. The – often younger – more technologically minded swore by the GPS watches, while the typically older, more traditional entrants stuck with their maps and compasses. Between them, there was a silent stand-off. It soon became apparent that how you found your way round the course was becoming more and more of a contentious issue within the mountain-running community. It came down to whether you thought an ability to navigate was at the heart of mountain running, or just an optional add-on.

It wasn't until a couple of high-profile race results ended up with one-sided results that things got properly stirred up. Poor visibility meant that podium places were basically determined by whether or not the top three used a GPS. With the cat truly among the pigeons, the FRA was forced to sort it out. After much heated debate, they deemed that going forward races would be classified as 'GPS' or 'non-GPS'. The 'non-GPS' category meant that such races would not allow runners to use a device that would show them their route or display their current position electronically. This was a game-changer.

In Northern Ireland, the iconic Annalong Horseshoe race was one of the first to adopt this 'Non-GPS' status. Just to drill home the seriousness of the matter, the race instructions stated that any person detected using

GPS equipment during the race would not only be disqualified, but also barred from entering the event for the next five years. If that wasn't enough to scare the wits out of non-navigators who wanted to run in such races, then nothing would.

I hoped that the GPS controversy would drum up a bit of business for my nascent company, and sure enough, as soon as I started advertising, mountain runners quickly started signing up. It was either that, or they had heard I had started the company when Pete got sick and they were giving me a sympathy vote. Regardless of their motivations, I got busy with preparing the course materials and sorting out potential dates.

I was very aware that, behind all this, I needed to practise group management skills for my Mountain Leader award. I didn't want, however, to have massive numbers on each course. The group had to be small enough that each person felt they had the time and space to ask whatever they wanted, no matter how stupid they thought their question was. After much thought, I settled on a maximum of three people for each session.

At the end of February, two months after Pete's death, I ran my inaugural course. Three amazing women signed up, two of them having journeyed all the way from Dublin to participate. I was genuinely touched. Though I had taught navigation before to people, this was the first time that it was on my terms. If they were nervous about participating, I was absolutely petrified.

'Welcome, welcome, welcome,' I said as cheerfully as I could. 'My name is Moire and I'm so happy that you've come along for our course.' I asked them to introduce themselves and to tell me what they wanted to learn. They all looked nervously at each other, unsure who wanted to admit their ignorance first. 'To navigate!' they soon all replied once the first one had plucked up the courage. All of them were already mountain runners. All of them had come a cropper at various times. They were sick and tired of getting lost, of being afraid of getting lost, and of not signing up for races because they were sure they'd get lost. It was a common theme.

Little did they know that whatever navigational error they had made, I had already made it ten times over. If they thought their sense of direction was bad, mine was infinitely worse. The only advantage was that I knew how powerful a map and compass could be to keep me right.

The problem with navigation courses I'd previously been on was that they were mostly designed for mountain walkers. Though the navigation tools they taught were great, many of them were overkill. I'd leave them feeling I'd learned so much, yet knowing the majority of the syllabus I couldn't apply to mountain-running scenarios. There was no way I was going to use pacing to take me off a summit when I was too tired to remember my name let alone count up to a hundred. I didn't give a damn about slope angle when I was more concerned about being caught by my nemesis on the final descent.

I was adamant that I wanted to spend as much time on the mountain with these course participants. As my impromptu flora and fauna lesson with Rachy showed, I'm a great fan of learning by doing as opposed to swotting up via textbooks. So as soon as I could, we headed out on to the hill.

'So where are we?' I asked the group before we'd even walked for a minute. All three heads plunged into their maps. 'Look up!' I shouted. 'Look around us. What can you see?'

'Forest.'

'A river.'

'This path.'

'A mountain.'

'Mountain!' I screamed in delight. 'Yes, a mountain! And as a mountain runner, that's the first thing we need to look for, the mountain bit.' It was a chance to wax lyrical about contours and how these should be a mountain runner's best friend.

I went easy on them for the first while and let them stick to the path. Mountain runners seem to have an amazing affinity to paths, loving them passionately, following them blindly even if they lead them over cliffs. We looked for little features along the trail, with me pointing them out on their maps before asking the group to find them for me in reality.

It might have been a lesson for mountain runners, but all this map reading and feature-finding was done at a walk.

'If you can't navigate while walking, there's no way you'll be able to do it while running,' I told them. 'Believe me, I've tried.' I was still scarred from some of the navigation mistakes I've made while running, which I could have easily avoided if only I'd slowed down.

Soon enough we left the path to follow one of the many walls that carved up the Mournes. With the wall going straight up the side of a mountain, it was a perfect opportunity to see how crossing contour lines drawn on a map felt in reality. I placed myself at the back of the group to make sure we stuck together, that no one felt that they were too slow or unfit for this section. I was the one who was going to come last. It was a small thing that I'd been told good group management involved.

When we got to the top, everyone seemed relieved we had put the climb behind us and had found where the contours levelled off.

'What's that mountain?' one participant asked me, pointing far into the distance. She was asking about Slieve Bearnagh, which we could just make out to the east. Its distinctive rock tors rose majestically above the surrounding peaks.

Though it was a legitimate question and gave us a nice learning point, it was also nice to just stop for a bit, to have a look around. It's not something mountain runners tend to do when they're out training or racing. We normally push and puff our way up the slope, and then turn around when we get to the top and run quickly back down again.

Pete used to always berate me for my inability to stop at summits when we went out into the mountains together.

'Can you not just sit down and take in the view?' he asked when we'd hit a cairn.

'But the descent is the fun part,' I'd protest, swivelling around swiftly to run back to where we'd come from. Maybe I should have sat down a bit more with him on mountaintops and appreciated what was around me rather than always rushing off to do the next thing.

We unfolded our maps to take a moment to work out which mountain was which. As my three students figured out the names, I decided to engage my most powerful group management technique.

'Sweeties anyone?' I shouted, pulling out a plastic bag from my rucksack and rattling it before their eyes. The oohs and aahs that came forth were heartening. I'd done well to steal the bags of sweets friends had left for my kids during house visits. In an effort to save their teeth, I'd inadvertently gained popularity with my clients. Double score.

Once we'd named all the mountains from the map, it was time for some compass work. The ladies looked at me with abject fear. It was the exact same look my eighty-year-old mother gave me when I presented her with a smartphone and told her it would revolutionise her life.

'Seriously, this compass will save your ass,' I promised. 'If you're on a misty summit and can't see which way to go, it'll point you in the right direction.' I took them through the couple of steps you need to do so that the needle and arrow are lined up correctly. I then got them to hit a tiny knoll to prove their compasses did indeed work.

When they all found themselves in the right place, smiles slowly crept across their faces. It was a beautiful sight, watching the penny drop with them all. I could feel their confidence grow. It was heartening.

While their compasses with their lines and arrows and dials were being slowly demystified, all I could think about were the amazing adventures these ladies were about to embark on. Understanding their contours and knowing how to use compasses was going to open up for them such a world of wondrous places. They just didn't know it yet. With a little more practice, they'd be able to visit valleys and cols and peaks that they never knew existed. I was so excited for them.

I gave them another few goes at setting their compass before telling them how, as a mountain runner, by pre-marking your map and preparing your bearings ahead of schedule, you can run faster and freer. It really wasn't rocket science, but it was just something that hadn't occurred to them before. The sound of more pennies dropping was audible.

My only worry through all this was that I was going to end up giving my navigation tricks of the trade away to some fast young un' some day, who was going to start beating me at my own game. But at the age of forty-three, having had some really good years of mountain-running behind me, I realised it was a risk I was willing to take.

We practised a couple more bearings and found some more map features on the ground before making our way back to the car park. Our return-journey chat turned to race plans and to people we mutually knew. The Irish mountain-running community is so close knit, our racing circuit is so small, that though we had never met each other until that day, we had loads of common ground.

It was lovely just being out there on the mountains with like-minded people, spending time doing something I loved. Yes, I was getting a QMD out of it, with a big dose of group management practice. But what was more important was I was getting a chance to share what I knew and to help others get into the sport I loved.

I continued to hold navigation courses as the weeks went on. I really enjoyed the work. Not only was it an income, but it also distracted me from all the noise of Pete's departure that I couldn't avoid as soon as I got back to civilisation. I'd slowly gotten used to not having him at home. I was becoming accustomed to single parenting. Unfortunately with a partner's death, and particularly when it's suicide, there is always something bigger waiting for you, preparing to pull you under just when you least expect it.

CHAPTER 16

A SCOTTISH EASTER

When a death is caused by suicide, the police have to get involved. Not only did they assist in the search for Pete the day he went missing, but they also had to coordinate a subsequent investigation into the cause of his death.

Though it was obvious to me that Pete had taken his own life, his demise was officially classified as sudden and unnatural. This meant that the coroner was tasked to undertake a post-mortem. They needed to be sure that Pete didn't die as a result of foul play. It was apparently standard procedure.

Given Pete's medical history, and from the informal conversations I had had with the police when visiting the place Pete was found, I knew no one else was involved in his death. So when the police asked me if I wanted an inquest to take place, I declined. I didn't think it was necessary to drag up and trawl through Pete's personal details in an open public forum.

I had also had too many horrible surprises over the preceding months. I was nervous an inquest would serve to throw something else unpleasant up, something upsetting that I didn't really need to know. At the end of the day, even if it did reveal something additional, an inquest would never bring Pete back. I felt there was no point having one.

Though I inevitably second-guessed some events, I did not blame myself.

Pete was a highly independent, intelligent man. He always knew his mind and could not be easily swayed. Our relationship was also based on profound for respect for one other and for each others' choices. It meant that, if Pete had decided to die, even if his disease had tarnished his ability to make good decisions, I knew that there was little I could have done to convince him otherwise.

The coroner apparently took my request into consideration when, at the beginning of April, three months after Pete died, I received a call from the police. They informed me that an inquest would not be held. I felt an immense sense of relief, as if I'd been released from a load I didn't even know I'd been carrying.

The decision not to proceed with an inquest meant that I could finally register Pete's death with the local registrar. This would allow me to obtain a death certificate, a document that would allow me to begin the process of accessing assets that were held in Pete's name. Not having a death certificate had been an administrative headache up until then, causing even more delays that added to my at times alarmingly high stress levels.

I visited the government office the day after the police call. No one else was present in the waiting room. I welcomed its emptiness. I didn't want people looking at me and wondering whose death I had come to register. I still felt embarrassed that I had 'lost' my husband. I didn't want people sitting there, staring at me, blaming me for such carelessness.

The registrar soon called me into her room to prepare Pete's certificate. I had brought Aran and Cahal along with me, and was heartened to see a stack of toys already in the corner of the office. My children were obviously not the only ones who had to disclose a death of a loved one. Others had gone before them and weathered this storm. My kids immediately delved into the box to leave me to conduct my business.

It was surreal making Pete's death so official. Maybe the lack of paperwork to date had let me pretend it wasn't true, that Pete was still working abroad somewhere and that he'd be back soon. My brain had been kind to me thus far, trying to cushion me from the blow.

The registrar was kind and courteous throughout, well versed in how to discuss such a delicate subject as death.

'What lovely boys,' she said. 'What ages are they?'

They were playing so quietly behind me, I had nearly forgotten they were there.

'Oh, three and five,' I replied. My stomach lurched as soon as I said how old they were. I didn't want sympathy for being a single mum of children so young, but knew that was what she was probably feeling. Even though she obviously meant well, her silent pity disempowered me.

I watched her type in the details required for each line of the certificate. For the 'place of death', she simply wrote 'in the vicinity' of our home. It was dignified, yet said it all. I couldn't help but regret that Pete never had the luxury of passing away in a caring hospital or in the privacy of his own bedroom, as he would if he had died of natural causes. And yet, I was eternally grateful to Pete for having quietly slipped out our door that morning, for not having done the deed within our house where I would have been the one to find him. I was also grateful to the police and Mountain Rescue, and had told them so, for having shouldered that burden instead.

'Would you like the long or short version?' the registrar asked me once she had completed the form.

'What's the difference?' I asked.

'The long version has the cause of death. The short one omits it.'

I went to speak, but my voice hesitated. I didn't want to have to make such a decision.

Then I thought about how helpful it had been in the past three months when I been open and honest with others, like when I had spoken to people at Pete's funeral and freely admitted that it had been depression that had led to his suicide. I thought about how, though I had told my children that their Daddy had gone to heaven, I had withheld from them the actual way that their Father had died. This particular omission grated on me, made me worry about what I would say to them, how I would say it, when I would say it, even though I knew they were still too young to hear how Pete's death had really occurred.

'Long version,' I eventually replied. With society telling us that we should speak more and more about mental health issues, I decided to take a stand right there and then, not to hide from the fact that Pete had taken his own life. That is how 'hanging' as cause of death ended up being written on Pete's certificate. I was well aware that I would hand this documentation to bankers, lawyers, secretaries and accountants, who would in turn see how their former client died. Maybe if they saw how stark this form of death is, I thought, something within themselves or within their own offices or homes might change for the better.

I registered Pete's death a couple of days before the kids got off school for their Easter holidays. There was something so final about having it engraved in black and white that made me suddenly feel grief; intense, horrible, soul-destroying grief. Over the previous few months, I had somehow managed to convince myself that I had emerged from the bereavement cycle relatively unscathed, and had happily landed at a mature and responsible acceptance of my loss. Holding Pete's death certificate in my hand officially proved me wrong. My initial acceptance had only been part of a momentary grace period. Now my grieving process had been slammed hard into a brutal accelerated reverse.

Fortunately I had already organised to go away with the boys for the Easter break. It served as a suitable distraction to the whirlwind I was suddenly swept up in. In the months before Pete fell ill, Pete and I had made a momentous decision to buy a campervan. We were tired of booking hotels, spending large sums of money on meals and flights for our young family if we wanted to go on holiday. If we were to have breaks with the boys, it made sense to be totally self-sufficient. There were plenty of beautiful places within Ireland and the UK that we could happily drive to. It would also allow us to go on mini-breaks of a night or two on the slightest whim. All we'd need to do was hop in and drive off.

We had spent nearly a year researching the best vehicle for us. We had quickly found that motorhomes were too big and bulky to negotiate Ireland's narrow rural roads. They also had too many buttons to press, which made them far too complicated. So, after much thought and asking around, we opted to get ourselves a basic Renault Trafic van and get it converted ourselves.

What came back from the garage was a thing of beauty. It had a gas cooker, sink and fridge so that we could cook and store our meals. It had front swivel seats and collapsible tables so that we eat together as a family. The roof popped up to reveal a double bed, while down below, the seats could flip down and rearrange to sleep another two. The *pièce de résistance* as I saw it was the space left for my bike. I considered it far too precious to hang off an outside carrier, so had insisted enough room was left at the back to store my bike safely inside.

Pete never got to go on holiday in our campervan. By the time it arrived, his persistent insomnia had already started. We didn't think it wise that he spent nights tossing and turning in the van's cooped up confines. We thought we'd leave such a holiday to another day, when Pete was feeling better. Such a trip never arrived.

Now that I had the campervan, I guessed I'd better put it to use. So I decided to book a ferry trip to Scotland over the Easter holidays with a plan to visit some friends while over there. Mostly, however, I intended to just drive around and find nice places to hang out. I was curious to see what campervan life was really about.

I paid the extra fee to make the ferry booking flexible. If the holiday all became a bit too much for us, we could just pack up the van and head back home on the next available sailing. I wasn't sure how we'd cope with the vacation, so didn't want the extra stress if we needed to cancel our plans last minute.

Before we headed off for our inaugural campervan holiday, Cahal decided that our campervan needed christening.

'Well what do you want to call it then?' I asked him as I packed up our duvets and pillows from our beds.

'Campervan is a girl,' he replied. 'I'm a boy, and Aran's a boy, and Tom's a boy, and Daddy was a boy. But you're a girl.'

'Okaaayyy,' I said, not sure where this was going. Three-year-olds have an amazing ability to go off on weird and wonderful tangents within conversations. Cahal appeared to be off on one of those adventures.

'So campervan has to be a girl,' he said. 'There are too many boys in the family.' Now I could understand his rationale.

'Any girl's name in particular?' I asked.

He went away and had a think, but only after I refused his suggestion of Ninja Warrior as a potential name.

'Dervla,' he said when he eventually came back. 'I have a girl called Dervla in my class.'

'Ok then,' I said, lifting him up into my arms and giving him a hug. 'Dervla Campervan it is.'

As we set off with Dervla to catch our ferry, Pete's absence felt acute. We had carefully installed four seats in our campervan, one for each of us. Now the front passenger seat beside me lay vacant. I had tried to at least pile it high with snacks to take away some of its emptiness, but it was not enough. Pete would have been our map reader, our DJ, our snack scoffer. No one was there now to do his in-car jobs.

I had decided to camp close to Stranraer that first night, so that I didn't have to contend with a long drive after our ferry ride from Belfast port. The place I had booked was perfect, a small farm with a campsite attached and all the necessary amenities. Even better was the fact that the sun was shining and the air was warm, despite it being only April. We parked the van and popped the roof before having a look around our base for the night. Cahal immediately spotted some chickens in the distance and decided to give chase. Aran took off in hot pursuit.

'Come back,' I shouted as they bolted across a road that ran straight through the centre of the campsite. I ran after them frantically, worried they would heedlessly cross it again and get knocked down in the process. Once I'd caught them, I pulled them both back to the vicinity of the van, their squeals reverberating around our pitch.

'You can't just run off like that!' I scolded. 'You're allowed to go as far as the end of our pitch and no further.' I wasn't convinced they were listening.

Just as I settled down inside the van to a well-earned beer from our perfectly chilled fridge, I heard another outbreak. Aran and Cahal were outside on the grass, beating the hell out of each other.

'Guys!' I shouted. 'Stop! Play nicely! Please!'

My request came too late as Cahal took a swing at Aran's head and landed a fearsome clout.

'For god's sake,' I said, bolting out of my chair. 'This is meant to be a holiday.'

Aran ran towards me in floods of tears, searching for a hug, pleading for me to put Cahal out of the family. All I could do in return was thank God I had booked a flexi-fare.

'Right lads,' I said, getting down on my knees to make sure they heard me clearly. 'You stop fighting right now or we're going home.' I was playing their bluff of course; I had no intention of packing up right then and there as I really wanted to finish my beer and perhaps down another. So I used the most serious, sombre voice I had, though deep down I wanted to screech at them as loud as I possibly could.

My over-reaction to their boys-will-be-boys play fighting wasn't helped by the fact that I was super stressed. Up until then, I had been putting on a good face, soldiering on with everything. Now that I was parked in a field with a beer in hand on 'holiday' with no distractions, I could acutely feel every bit of tension that had accumulated since Pete's illness and death.

Another few beers helped me finally settle down. The boys found somewhere safe to play, and we thankfully managed to survive our first night living in Dervla Campervan.

The next morning we packed up for the three-hour drive to Edinburgh. My friend, Avril, lived there and was ready to host us for Easter weekend.

I knew Avril from my time living in Kenya more than a decade before. When I moved back to Ireland she had put me in contact with her brother, Paul, who in turn introduced me to the sport of mountain running. I was looking forward to seeing her again after all this time.

Avril was in full-on Easter preparation mode when we arrived. She told the boys that the Easter bunny had been spotted in the neighbourhood and was bound to visit them soon. She had also boiled eggs all ready for painting and rolling down Arthur's Seat, a celebrated Edinburgh Easter tradition apparently. Aran and Cahal could barely contain their excitement. According to them, the prospect of arts and crafts combined with choco-late eggs made this the best campervan holiday ever.

While Avril's own children took the boys off to entertain them, Avril sat down with me in her garden armed with a bottle of Prosecco.

'I sometimes forget that others are also grieving,' I said to Avril as she poured me a glass. I told her how I was recently chatting with a friend of Pete's about my late husband, thinking I was sharing a cool little anecdote. Instead of nodding and laughing along, I just saw tears welling up in his eyes. 'I can get so focused on myself and the boys that at times I forget there is a whole pile of people out there that miss Pete too.'

'It must be comforting to know that he meant so much to so many people,' Avril said.

'I suppose so,' I replied, swinging idly on her sun-seat. 'But what I just don't get is how there are people who weren't even that close to Pete who seem to grieve a lot, at times quite publicly.' Avril said nothing, gracefully allowing me to speak my mind. Just like with Louise, it was cathartic to talk with someone who had known me for so long. 'Like I know some of these people and what Pete really thought of them. Sometimes I just want to scream, "But you weren't even a good friend to him!'" I had recently heard the term 'grief vultures' used to describe such sorts.

'Maybe they feel guilty for missing out on the relationship they could have had,' Avril finally said. I knew she was right, that their inexplicable grief was probably born out of other struggles. Conceding this didn't make it any less annoying though.

The conversation continued until late, providing me with a space to voice my concerns out loud, allowing me to release them and exorcise them. At other times, vocalising my thoughts allowed me to see them and judge them in the cold light of day, forcing me to accept that some were actually untrue or unkind. Avril skilfully challenged me when she heard these unfounded notions, suggesting alternative ways of seeing and understanding all that was going on.

While catching up with a long-time friend and drinking Prosecco together proved incredibly healing, getting in touch with someone I had only briefly spoken with, but never met before, also proved therapeutic. The mountain runner and author, Jonny Muir, also lives in Edinburgh. We happened to share the same publisher and had touched base with each other when our books were released within months of each other. When I got in contact with him and told him I was in the area, he suggested we went for a run together in the northerly Pentlands, a hilly area I'd heard of but never visited.

Jonny pulled up in his car outside of Avril's house early on Easter Sunday morning. I recognised him from his Instagram and Twitter posts. They say you should never meet someone you've only seen on the Internet, but I thought I could make an exception in this case. We made small talk as we drove the short distance to Hillend.

'Please don't run too fast,' I pleaded as soon as we stepped out of his car. 'I'm really unfit these days.'

Between us, Jonny and I had completed four out of the five big mountain-running Rounds. While I had covered the Wicklow Round south of Dublin and the Denis Rankin Round in Northern Ireland's Mourne Mountains, Jonny had finished England's Bob Graham and Scotland's Charlie Ramsay. The fitness I had when completing those Rounds had long gone, however, ever since my aversion to training had kicked in.

Jonny was happy enough to slow his pace to allow the chat to flow.

'Have you seen the Wicklow Round record tumbled recently?' I said as we jogged up the first hill. The previous week, Paddy O'Leary had smashed the record by over forty minutes. As we spoke, Shane Lynch was out on the course right at that minute and word online was that he was ahead of Paddy's splits. Later that evening, Shane was to take the record off Paddy by just three minutes.

'It's great to see people running that quick,' Jonny replied as the incline steepened and we started to power walk. 'But for me, the Rounds are more than just about fast times. They're about the average mid-pack runner who trains hard, does their recces, prepares well, waits for the right weather and completes in just under twenty-four hours. I think what they get out of the Rounds is just as, if not more, impressive.'

I silently agreed with him. I knew what I personally got out of doing the Rounds was far more important than a time recorded against my name. Your personal gains, however, aren't always as exciting to speak about. They rarely make the web forum news or Facebook feeds.

We ran on over the hills, with Edinburgh spreading out beneath our feet. It reminded me of the unparallelled views of Ireland's capital from the Dublin

Mountains. I loved the way that we were so removed from the goings-on of a major city, yet still so close to them.

'Well done on the book,' I said, trying to keep up with Jonny as he bounded down the path towards our second peak. 'Fantastic read.'

'Thanks,' he said. 'People have given me some nice feedback.' Jonny's book, *The Mountains are Calling* had traced the history of Scottish hill running, with many in-depth interviews with some of the most formidable athletes in our sport. He told me how hard it was to gain access of some these figures, so reclusive and humble these mountain-running legends tend to be. Our conversation soon diverted off into writers' speak; there was talk of cover design and editing processes, of publicity quotes and social media campaigns. And just to give something for our publisher to repost, we paused for a moment on one of the hilltops and took a quick selfie.

As we turned around to start the journey back, our conversation changed to things closer to home. There is something about running in the wide-open mountains that allows talk to flow to topics that indoor spaces place barriers on. I felt comfortable speaking to Jonny of Pete's death, while he in turn shared how he was soon to become a father for a third time, life somehow coming full circle. We spoke of things we still hoped to do with our lives and people who inspired us to achieve them.

Our ninety-minute run may have been brief, but it was rich with meaning.

'Will you write about your loss?' Jonny asked me as we drove back to Avril's place.

'I don't know,' I replied. 'Maybe. Maybe not.'

Everything was still so raw, still so unprocessed that I didn't even know where to start. All I knew was that, when I'd written before, I had felt compelled to put my experience into words. When I had put pen to paper before, it was because I thought I had something to say that might help someone somewhere in a similar situation. Right then and there, I was glad I didn't have such a compulsion. I simply didn't have the energy to write. The state I was in, I wasn't sure I could be of much help to anyone.

After bidding farewell to Jonny, and then Avril, I drove away to the western coast, to spend time alone with my boys. We parked Dervla on the windswept coast near Arisaig, looking out towards the solitary islands of Rum and Eigg in the distance. For three whole days we slept, walked, swam, ate and played. It was the type of holiday Pete and I had envisaged, yet ultimately one that only I would fulfil.

On the beach one morning I took a photo of myself with the kids. Looking back at it, we all looked happy, relaxed by our time away. The only thing I regret was, in that photo, our unit looked so small. There was no Pete standing behind us. I hoped the boys would grow quickly, so that they could fill the gap in our photo frame.

Through this poignant sadness, I recalled my Kenyan friend Louise's advice, for me to make new memories. On those Scottish sandy shores, I resolved to rebuild a new life with Aran and Cahal, a life that would always be in memory of our dearest Pete.

CHAPTER 17

PARENTS UP PEAKS

I got straight back into work with Happy Out Adventures after our return from Scotland. Bookings were coming through nicely, the non-GPS race rule obviously scaring enough mountain runners into learning how to navigate. After each of the courses, I'd send out a short feedback survey, to see what went well, what didn't go so well, and if there was anything else they'd like to learn.

Trying to keep an ear out for what people wanted was important during these early months of operation. It spurred me on to develop an advanced navigation course for those who wanted to go further off-trail, to compete in the likes of mountain marathons. It made me think of road runners who weren't too sure about how to even begin to run on mountains and how I could help them.

One evening I gave a talk at Tollymore National Outdoor Centre about how I got into the sport of mountain running and the adventures I had had, many of which were made possible by Pete being at my side. I also spoke about how I was now teaching others to navigate. Afterwards a lady came up to me. Ian, her husband, was a well-known international mountain runner who I guessed had dragged her along to the event. She introduced herself as Anna.

'Do you just take people out to teach them the basics?' Anna asked me, looking a little shy. 'It's just that, I don't mountain run. Like, don't get me wrong. I *definitely* don't want to mountain run. I only want to bring my children out into the hills.'

I wanted to reach out and hug her. This was what the Mountain Leader award was all about – to help others journey safely in the uplands.

'Of course, that's no problem at all, I can do basics,' I said. 'What would you like to learn?'

Anna told me how she lived locally, with the Mourne Mountains right on her doorstep. Despite how close they were, she didn't feel confident enough to go into them without her mountain-running husband in tow. She knew it was a wasted opportunity.

'I really want to get my kids used to going into the outdoors,' she explained. 'I know it'd be good for them. In fact, it would also do me the world of good.'

I listened to her simple request, to learn enough so that she could safely bring her boys on a couple of child-friendly mountain routes at weekends. It was totally do-able.

I advertised this 'Parents up Peaks' course soon after, with another local lady, Marion, taking up the other place. We met in the heart of the Mourne Mountains, at Ott car park on a weekday morning when our kids were all in school. There was not another soul in sight.

Having already heard what Anna wanted to learn, I asked Marion what she hoped to get out of the day.

'My husband works in the army, so knows how to read maps and everything,' Marion explained. 'It means when we're outdoors I always leave him to it. But he's often away for work, so if I want to go on my own, or with the kids, I can't.' I was starting to hear a common thread.

If I ever find the person who started the rumour that women can't navigate, they'd better watch their back. Anna and Marion were not the first, and will not be the last, females who swore to me their male counterparts were better placed to take charge of the map. This gender-biased belief that I was being told over and over was highly frustrating to hear. Fortunately I knew, and had indeed seen, otherwise. I had in fact witnessed, with my very own eyes, men also getting horribly lost.

Even during my mountain-running courses I had seen a marked difference during initial introductions between how the men and women described their perceived navigational abilities. Most men would tell me they knew a bit, had done a bit, would like to learn a bit more. On the other hand, the women would go to great pains to describe to me in vivid detail an example of how their innate stupidity had caused them to get irretrievably lost on a mountain range. They would use this as proof to me that they were not good enough or smart enough to trust themselves with a map and compass. They said they desperately needed my help.

I would derive great pleasure in redressing these perceptions while out on the mountainside with them. I would enjoy seeing the women follow simple navigation rules I'd give them, observing them religiously before suddenly realising they knew exactly where they were and where they were going. It was blissful to watch them grow in confidence as I slowly revealed that they really weren't as stupid as they thought.

Even though I didn't mean to, most male participants ended getting a bit of a dressing down. As they wandered off in a random direction, I was forced to reveal to them that they probably didn't know as much as they had originally made out.

'You are heading in exactly the opposite direction to the rest of us because you aligned your bezel's orienting arrow south instead of north,' I'd have to point out. 'If you keep following your needle instead of your direction of travel arrow, you're going to end up in the North Pole.'

Back at Ott car park, I assured Anna and Marion that their ability to have babies did not automatically render them forever navigationally impaired. I then spent the first half an hour going over the basics of map symbols and scales as well as how to orientate a map. Then we took another half an hour to look at safety issues before they'd even head out into mountain terrain. We discussed weather, clothing, food, emergency equipment and route planning, giving them a simple guide to take away and use the next time they embarked on their own mountain walk.

With these basics covered, we headed out on to the hills.

'I hope we're not going to go too fast,' Anna and Marion chimed practically in unison as we crossed over the stile, before both explaining to me how unfit they were.

First they had told me how useless they were at navigating. Now, before we had even started our walk, they were making excuses in case I thought they were going too slow.

I would have given off to them for making excuses, only for the fact that I knew I was also guilty of doing the same. Wasn't the first thing I said to Jonny before our Pentlands run out of Edinburgh was that I was unfit and couldn't run that fast? What is it with us ladies that we have to constantly apologise for our perceived inabilities, that we've such a crisis in self-belief?

I assured Anna and Marion that we were out to enjoy ourselves and that we'd go at a leisurely pace. I had already planned that, if someone thought they had to speed up to prove a point to themselves or even to me, I'd stop us all dead in our tracks, make sure everyone caught up before delivering some mountain-related fact. I was already well rehearsed to give an in-depth talk on the heathers that were starting to bloom across the hills. With the Mourne Mountains being one of the few habitats in Ireland where all three heather types are found, I was looking forward to pointing out the plump cross-leaved heath and the bell heather that were beginning to flower. Their pink and purple hues were a welcome relief from the brown and beige bogland that had dominated the landscape over the winter months. We were still too early in the year to see ling with its small, pretty purple bouquets decorating the length of their stems, but at least this proliferous heather would persist up until October, bringing some much needed colour to the hills as winter loomed.

If my heather talk failed to excite, I'd prepared as a back-up a riveting discourse on the small, bright yellow tormentil flowers that were also littering the ground. Back in the day, tormentil was used to tan leather when Ireland was lacking trees. My favourite use, however, was its ability to treat diarrhoea, a handy property if you found yourself stuck on one of the Mournes' many cliffs and were literally shitting yourself about getting back down.

Anna, Marion and I hiked up the path towards the Mourne wall, keeping a close eye on our maps. Once we'd crossed the stile, we headed towards Loughshannagh Mountain, a summit located at 617 metres above sea level. I wanted them to experience what it felt like to ascend to such a height. I kept the pace slow, but we were still puffing and panting a little as we finally reached the top.

'How did that feel?' I asked as we congregated around the cairn.

'Good,' Anna replied. 'Tough though,' as she stood to catch her breath.

I explained to them that we had set out at 379 metres above sea level, the height of Ott car park, so had really only climbed 238 metres in total.

'So if Slieve Donard is 853 metres high, about four times what we've just done, do you think you'll bring your kids up that?'

Anna and Marion laughed nervously, before shaking their heads. Their definitive answer was no.

Slieve Donard is Northern Ireland's highest mountain, found within the Mourne Mountains. A wide trail runs all the way from the coastal town of Newcastle to its very top. With its iconic status and well-trodden path, it is a popular suggestion for day trips. The comeuppance was that I'd seen families frog-marching their young children towards its summit. Many had no food or water or proper footwear or raingear. The kids looked knackered, bedraggled, even scared. Ascending the mountain on a whim for a fun family outing was a really bad idea. I was hoping to drum into people that, if you wanted to put your kids off the outdoors for life, your first family hike should definitely be up and down Slieve Donard.

'It's lovely up here, isn't it?' Anna said, taking in the view. The sun was shining, the sky was blue, and we could see every one of the Mournes' formidable peaks laid out before us. Down below, the waters of Lough Shannagh glistened in the mountain light. The deafening silence from this vast expanse felt almost meditative. I couldn't help but agree. 'I really wish I could get out and do this kind of thing more.'

'But you know how it is,' Marion said to us both. 'You just end up being too busy. It's hard making the effort to come out here.'

I also agreed with Marion. Especially after having my own kids, there always seemed to be something going on at home that meant I couldn't leave. If I wanted to get out into the mountains, I really had to make the effort. This was hard at times.

Fortunately I had an advantage over Marion and Anna. I had previously lived in countries where there were no mountains, or no access to them. I could recall how my soul slowly died in such places. A two-year stint in the floodplains in Cambodia eroded away much of my joy. I became so deeply unhappy that by the end of my work assignment I practically ran out of the country. I also once did a short stint in Afghanistan. I was enthralled by its vast mountain ranges, but so deflated by the security protocols that strictly forbid us from setting foot in them. Now that I lived right beside the Mournes, I was very aware of how exceptionally lucky I was. I felt nothing but the deepest gratitude. In doing so, I also felt duty bound to make the most of them when others weren't as fortunate, for all those poor people stuck in Cambodia and Holland and Denmark and other similar flat-lands.

We had such a great view of the mountains all around us that I figured it was a good place to sit down.

'Brownies anyone?' I said as we made ourselves comfortable on the random stones strewn across the summit. I unbuckled my rucksack to reveal a zip-lock bag containing blobs of home-baked gooey chocolatey mess. I was blessed by the fact that people become less fussy about appearances in the mountains. No one refused the oddly cut squares roughly wrapped up in cling-film.

'These are good!' Marion exclaimed once she'd had a taste. 'Can you send us the recipe?'

'Not a bother,' I replied. 'Personally I find that if you throw enough butter, sugar and chocolate at anything, it has to taste good.'

We sat there munching on our mid-trek snack, not giving a damn about the vast number of calories we were consuming. We deserved the treat. I felt happy just sitting there, taking in the space and sounds and serenity that I for some reason only ever experience in the mountains.

'If you're bringing your kids out into the mountains,' I said, continuing on with our lesson, 'you might want to think about what snack or treat you want to bring along. Like my boys always talk about how they used to go with their daddy to the beach and eat ice-cream together.'

It was just a casual remark, something I'd heard the boys say in recent days as the summer slowly beckoned, something I thought might be useful to share with Anna and Marion. It was a happy memory for Aran and Cahal, eating Cornettos on the beach with their father. I wanted to let Anna and Marion know how eating yummy food in the outdoors can help make good, lasting memories with your kids.

Only my remark was met with awkward silence, something I hadn't anticipated. I had spoken of Pete's death at the talk that Anna had attended, so she obviously knew the score. And I hadn't hidden the fact from other forums, so it was quite possibly the case that Marion was also aware. Should I have forewarned them I was going to speak of the dead? Immediately I felt guilty for putting them in the position where they didn't know what to say. It wasn't their fault, just a terrible societal hang-up that means that most of us don't know how to speak to others about death or grief, too worried that we might do or say the wrong thing.

The crazy thing about walking together with others in the mountains for a couple of hours, the more we do it, the more something within us opens up. I'll never understand truly why. Maybe it's the fact of doing exercise together, yet I have never had such deep and meaningful conversations while on a bike club spin or joint road run. Or is it simply because we bottle up so much these days that the mountains are one of the only remaining safe places where we feel that we can let these things out? Is it because, when faced with these gigantic peaks and empty valleys, we become so starkly aware of how small, how fragile, how temporary we are that we realise that these seemingly colossal concerns and worries and fears we have don't really matter in the scheme of things?

Maybe that is why I had shared with people I had only met that morning about Pete and the beach ice-cream. For me, after an hour of walking together in the highlands, it didn't feel like a big deal. I was well used to the cathartic effect the mountains can have on me.

As I continued taking parents up the Mournes' peaks throughout that year, some participants soon started experiencing this same effect. Though the first half of the course I'd concentrate on safety and navigation, the return journeys to the car park often ended up morphing into informal group-sharing sessions. I was moved by these strangers who felt comfortable telling me their deeply personal stories. Many of these tales related to why they had even come on such a course, why they felt more than ever the need to be in the great outdoors. Some told me about how they had previously experienced the transformative effect of the mountains when they were younger, and how they wanted to re-engage with this. Some people told me of worrying health issues that they thought being in the mountains could help resolve. Others spoke of being parents to children whom they felt the need to reconnect with.

Regardless of what was said or learned during those sessions, my abiding memory of all those courses was everyone arriving back at their cars with happy smiles. It was less an endorsement of the course, and more the fact that we all appreciated having spent time in the mountains with kindred spirits. It was also an expression of the excitement everyone had doing similar journeys and sharing similar joy within their own families.

I was also personally transformed during that time. By hanging up my mountain-running shoes for a while, by opting to travel at a walking pace, I was developing a different appreciation for the mountains and its people. Maybe what I most needed in my life right then, to help me with everything that was going on, was just to slow down a little.

CHAPTER 18

HONEST FUN

I kept putting my hiking boots on instead of my running shoes as I continued to prepare for my Mountain Leader award. Over the Easter holidays, Rachy had sat her five-day assessment, passing with flying colours. Despite being qualified and in no need of further practice, she agreed to still come out on the slopes to help me prepare for mine.

Soon another mountain-leader wannabe like me, Cara, joined us on our outings. I had met Cara at the talk I had given at Tollymore National Outdoor Centre, so she knew my deal. Cara's speciality was preparing and putting Duke of Edinburgh groups through their paces during overnight expeditions. Though she didn't need the award to continue doing this type of work, Cara considered the piece of paper nice to have, a validation of the skills she already possessed.

As we walked up towards the steep cliffs of Spellack for some steep ground and rope work, Cara and I grilled Rachy on her recent assessment. We wanted to know where she went, what she was asked, and what the assessors did if you made a mistake during those five long days of scrutiny. We had already heard horror stories from other assessments. We were hoping to dispel some of those myths. Someone had told me that the two-night expedition was the coldest and wettest they'd ever been in their life. Cara had heard frightening tales about night navigation tasks set that would have been difficult to carry out even in broad daylight.

The sun was shining and the Mournes looked particularly splendid that day. It didn't seem like work in the slightest as we dropped our rucksacks at the top of one of Spellack's many cliffs. Just above us the clouds drifted lazily across a piercing blue sky. The picture-perfect views we had were spectacular.

'Ok if I go first?' Cara said as we peered over the steep drop before us. I was happy to sit there and enjoy the first warmth of the year if Cara was willing to volunteer.

As Cara unravelled her rope I pulled out some home-baked goods. They say if life gives you lemons, make lemonade. I prefer to think, if your bananas get black and bruised, make banana cake. While I sunbathed and munched on my snack, Rachy, ready and willing as ever, agreed to be Cara's client and the one to descend the rock first.

I sat and watched Cara carefully set up her anchor and prepare Rachy's waist loop before positioning herself near the edge. She was doing things slightly differently from what Rachy and I normally did, and I thought her rig-up was particularly clever. It was becoming clear to me that if I headed out with different people, there was always something new to learn. Looking back at that time, I realise that constantly discovering new things about the mountains and its environment served to distract me, albeit momentarily, from all that was going on at home.

Out on Spellack Mountain that day, there was also something so freeing about being there with two other strong women, when women aren't supposed to be that independent or brave. It was wonderfully liberating being out with Cara and Rachy, all of us just hanging tough.

Once we had all practised lowering each other down, we agreed to each do an emergency abseil to get us off the cliff and back onto the flatter land below.

Rachy this time agreed to go first. She strung herself up tightly in a type of abseil configuration known as the 'South African', two strands of rope first under her armpits then crossed at the back, before being finally looped between her legs. Once she was trussed up like a turkey, Rachy leaned slowly backwards to start the descent. Only that, as soon as Rachy was half-way down this section, she realised there was nowhere to place her feet. The vertical rock just disappeared.

'Just take a little jump,' Cara suggested, calling over the edge to Rachy. 'That'll get you down.'

I saw the rope hop up, then drop, before Rachy let out a massive roar.

'Fuuuuuck!' Rachy cried out from below. I rushed to the edge, not sure I wanted to see the aftermath. Next thing I heard Rachy shouting, 'I've just gone and given myself a massive wedgie!'

It was enough to make me burst out laughing, the type of infectious laughter that makes your belly hurt. Cara couldn't help but join in. Rachy, for some reason, didn't find it quite as hilarious. I secretly wondered if this 'South African' abseil technique should be rechristened henceforth a 'Brazilian.'

After Pete's death, I had worried that I had lost much of my capacity for joy and fun. I often thought others would criticise me if I wasn't permanently sad. But out on the mountains, where only Rachy and Cara could see and hear me, I was totally free to laugh out loud.

Pete and I had some really good times together. Sometimes with death, and particularly with suicide, you feel like you're not allowed to celebrate the fun you had with that person. It seemed like no one wanted to ask me anymore, for example, how Pete and I met, in case recalling such happy memories made me cry. I felt like I wasn't allowed to talk about how he proposed to me in Dublin's Heuston Railway Station, down on one knee, with the ticket-selling ladies wolf whistling behind their screens before calling me over so that they could check out the bling. But such silence, such a moratorium on speaking about Pete, does a huge disservice to the amazing time we did have when he was still alive.

Having watched Rachy abseil down, I decided to wrap myself up with a classic rig instead of a South African. I was hoping the change in technique would cause a different part of my body, more my neck and shoulders as opposed to my fanny, to suffer from friction burns.

When all of us were back on terra firma, I looked at my watch. I couldn't believe it – we had already been out there for nearly three hours. The time had flown by.

'I gotta head,' I said, making my apologies. 'My kids get out of school soon.' Rachy also had plans to meet up with some of her rock-climbing mates elsewhere, so she agreed to walk out with me.

'I think I'll stay and practise some more while I'm here,' Cara replied. Both Rachy and I couldn't help envy her. The weather was warm and the hills were still. It was a perfect day to hang out in the Mourne Mountains.

'Whose is the ring?' I said to Rachy as we started our hike towards the road head. I had noticed her wearing it on a cord around her neck when we were busy doing our rope work. It was a new addition to her jewellery.

'It's my mum's,' Rachy replied. 'She passed away in January this year.' I had heard of Rachy's loss indirectly from others as her bereavement had happened before we had come to know each other. It meant that I had never properly offered my condolences. 'I asked my family if I could have her ring, to remember her, and I'm really lucky they agreed.'

Before Pete's death, I would have probably left the conversation at that. I may have even felt embarrassed that I'd asked about the ring in the first place. But having also been bereaved so recently, I didn't feel awkward talking more about her mum.

'Were you close?' I asked.

'In my twenties, no, not at all. I was struggling with loads of personal things,' Rachy said. 'I refused to let her in. But when I hit my thirties I finally resolved some of those issues, and my Mum finally understood. Like there was a moment where she really *got* me.'

'So you were close what, for the last five years?'

'Yeah, pretty much,' Rachy replied. 'And then she was diagnosed with leukaemia only two years ago. It was like we had finally reached a whole new level of understanding and then it was suddenly ripped away from us.'

'That really sucks,' I said. 'You must really miss her.'

'Big time,' Rachy replied without hesitation. 'She was like my rock. If I ever had any big decisions to make in life, or even if I just needed some tough love, she was the one I'd talk to. I miss having her around.'

I asked her how her family were coping and Rachy was happy to share. I equally told her about Pete's depression and how my own family was doing. It was healing common ground.

'You know, it's really important to respect other people's way of grieving,' Rachy said, as we picked our way carefully over the rutted mountain terrain towards the main trail. 'But I want to celebrate the good times I had with Mum and with Gavin, my cycling buddy, instead of focusing on the obvious tragic side. At the end of the day, I'm still here,' Rachy continued.

'Gavin took a hit for us that day on our bikes and I am alive because of him. If I let my life go down the pan, I feel like that would be a major insult to him.'

I nodded quietly. I agreed with her philosophy.

'I wonder though,' I said, 'if all this mountain-leader training hasn't come at the right time for both of us.' One of the things I had learned when being in the mountains and the emphasis of leadership within the award was that honesty and clarity were everything. In the same way, being able to talk openly about our losses proved good for both Rachy and me.

'I suppose being in the outdoors does force you to say how you feel or where you're at head-wise,' Rachy replied. 'Like if you don't admit you're suffering, you can end up in a situation where someone could potentially get hurt or die.'

When Pete was ill I thought a lot about what the mountains had taught me over the years. Often when he was faced with another dilemma that his depression had dragged up, I'd resort to telling Pete about something scary that had happened to me in the mountains and that, in the end, had turned out well.

I was frequently dragged back to that day during the 2017 Mourne Mountain Marathon where I was convinced I was going to die. It was day two of the event and my team-mate Paul and I were tired after a first day of hard racing. Our brains were fuddled from a night of not sleeping in a cold tent in a wind-swept field, and we were just looking forward to getting that day's course done and reaching the finish. The fact that we weren't thinking straight was all part of the race's challenge.

We had collected the first two controls quite easily and, with our choice of route being up to us, had decided how we would journey to the third.

Only that, as we started to go in the direction we'd agreed on, we saw other teams running off in a different way.

Paul and I had already discounted the way they were all going when we had originally planned our route. There were close together contour lines with thick black lines where they were headed, a sure sign of steep rocky ground. It didn't look safe on the map. The only thing was that there were at least three other teams going in that direction. Some of these teams comprised international orienteers who could read maps exceptionally well; other teams had locally-based, well-seasoned runners who knew these mountains like the backs of their hands. So, despite our well-made plan, I suggested to Paul that we blindly followed them. They couldn't all be wrong, surely?

We were travelling from the control at Cove Lough towards our next one on Slieve Beg. In between the lake and that summit, in the direct line of travel, lay Upper Cover with its multiple cliffs. I assumed the other teams knew a secret passageway through these rock faces, even though there was nothing indicated on the map.

Before we knew it, we were all crag-fast. Below us was a vertical drop of ten metres, enough to put an end to your race if you fell off it. In front of us were cliffs that could not be crossed. It made total sense to double back. The only problem with turning around and retracing our steps was the amount of time we'd lose. Faced with this potential loss, and with blinkered race heads on all of us, the teams decided to climb up. Paul and I stupidly followed.

I have no head for heights. Suffice to say that if there was ever a time when I needed anti-diarrheal tormentil flowers, it was then. I was petrified.

'Paul, seriously, I need to go back down,' I said, trying to calm the quiver in my tone.

'You'll be fine,' he replied from above. 'Just place your hands and feet where I put mine.' I looked up and saw some of the other teams negotiating the steep terrain with ease. Those who were coping well were part-time rock climbers, so were well at home on Upper Cove's cliffs.

Looking up at where the others were going and listening to what Paul was telling me to do helped me get through that near-death moment. It made me fix my eyes in front of me, to just think about the next step and only that. It stopped me looking down and seeing the frightening drop that would kill me if I fell. It was like a dress rehearsal for how I'd cope in the immediate aftermath of Pete's death.

When we finally emerged on to the plateau approaching Cove Mountain's cairn, I was close to tears.

'I need a hug,' I said to Paul, so traumatised was I from that impromptu rock-climbing event.

'I was worried too,' he said. 'I thought you'd freak out and not make it.' I hadn't realised that he had held it together for my sake. Out of gratitude, I shared him with my rationed chocolate supply that was exclusively reserved for emergencies.

'Bad things happen, but we can get through this together,' I'd say to Pete. 'Sure I'm only standing here today alive and well because of my team-mate. I'm here for you too, you know.' When this encouragement I gave Pete came to nothing, I'd become a little more prescriptive. 'You need to do what your doctors and counsellor say,' I told him. 'You're not in a position to work this out alone. Just put your head down, listen to those who know better, like I did on that mountain. Do exactly what they say. You'll get better then.'

When I told Pete other traumatic mountain stories of where I'd got out of some hairy moment by the skin of my teeth, I noticed that he had no reciprocal tales to tell. It was like Pete had been so smart that he had always been able to see trouble coming before anyone else did. He would then either fix the problem or make a pre-emptive, strategic move to get the hell out of its path. The result was he had never really struggled at anything. He had lived a gifted life. So when I asked him to be patient, to entrust himself to others, to believe things that were outside his control would get better, he had no experience of doing exactly that.

I'll be forever haunted by Pete's final words to me the morning that he left. I was telling him again that everything would be okay, that he'd get better one day, that we'd get through this together. He shook his head and said with such sorrow, 'You're so strong.' If only he knew how wrong he was, how his depression had made him believe yet another fallacy.

If anything, my mountain experiences had not made me strong. They had instead exposed to me how incredibly fragile I am.

I am brutally aware that I need to be careful out in the mountains and look after myself in case they throw their worst at me. I had also learned the hard way that I need others even if I want to appear independent and brave. I had needed Paul's help on Cove Mountain to rescue me from its unforgiving cliffs.

I've also learned how fickle the mountains can be, how quickly things change out there, and how life can mirror that unpredictability. There is only so much I can control in the mountains and I've brought that lesson back home with me into my daily life.

What made Pete's statement also so wrong was that his depression had broken me. I felt the exact opposite of strong. I felt embarrassed to admit that I was destroyed when it was not I who was suffering from the disease. But I found out that being a constant carer for someone who is depressed turns out also to be very depressing.

If there was anything his disease proved to me, however, was that I had some sort of resilience. I was bruised, battered, terrified by this illness, but still got up every morning and tried to help him get well again. Saying that I was strong suggests that it didn't affect me, but the truth is that it did. Being resilient, however, meant I got back up every time I was beaten down by this mental illness that was borne by a loved one.

I've also lived a gifted life like Pete. I've never found myself wanting for food, warmth, safety or company. I've had a comfortable upbringing devoid of so many hardships. It's the type of life that doesn't lend itself to learning and practising resilience. But, thanks to my years spent roaming the mountains, I've swotted up on resilience. I know that if I'm cold and wet and tired and hungry, I can't just sit down on the nearest stone and give up. If I'm tempted to call it a day and phone Mountain Rescue to come get me, I mightn't even have battery or signal strength. I've often been faced with no choice but to get myself to safety. If resilience is about keeping going despite adversity then, thanks to the mountains, I'd concede I've learned that lesson.

CHAPTER 19

SCATTERED

It wasn't until the end of May, five months after his passing, that I finally spread Pete's ashes. I had spent the intervening time wondering about the most appropriate way. All I knew was that however I did it, it had to be meaningful to me. I had sat through his funeral, the crematorium ceremony and the month's mind mass, traditions where Irish Catholic families say farewell to their dead. The familiarity of the structure, the signs, the prayers provide a safe harbour for mourners after the vicious storm of a loved one's death.

I, however, had come to crave something more personal, something that used both words and silence that purely represented what Pete and I had together. I wanted to use this opportunity to say my own goodbye. Fortunately his family allowed me to take charge of Pete's final request and let me carry it out as I saw fit.

Pete hadn't stipulated exactly where in the Comeraghs he wanted his ashes placed. I'm not sure he realised that there was such a large choice of venues when it came down to it. Did he want his ashes spread beside Lough Moyra, where he used to play and swim with his siblings during long hazy summer days? Did he want to be released at the summit of Knockanaffrin, for him to spread his wings from the range's highest peak? Or did he want them to be placed at the base of the mountain range so that everyone could easily visit them?

Fortunately a childhood friend of Pete's heard of my dilemma and came to my aid. He suggested a place high up on the Comeraghs' ridgeline, on a lesser-known peak I wasn't familiar with. From the spot he was suggesting, on the cultivated plateau below, you could just make out the farm where Pete grew up. You could see also Pete's younger brother's house at the end of its laneway, as well as Pete's friend's own bungalow. It meant that all of Pete's nearest and dearest could look up and see Pete's final resting place from the comfort of their own homes. I agreed with him. Pete would probably want to hang out right there.

When it came to deciding who would accompany me to such a ceremony, I reflected for a long while. Initially I wanted to invite my closest mountain-running friends to join me for an out and back run along the ridge, spreading Pete's ashes on the turn-around. The more I thought about this plan, the more my gut told me that it was wrong.

Throughout our many years together, Pete and I had spent so much quality time alone. We had been friends, lovers, husband and wife. So much of our lives had only involved the two of us. I didn't want to have yet another ceremony where there were other people mourning, expressing their own unique brand of sadness at losing a family member, a colleague or a friend. I wanted a moment where I could remember a partner who was so dearly missed. There was no one else on earth except me who could relate to Pete in this way.

I also didn't want to have to hold back my emotions during this ritual. I wanted the freedom to laugh or cry or scream, without wondering or worrying what those around me would think. I wanted for once to have some privacy while I remembered and celebrated him.

So I decided to run up to that place that Pete's childhood friend told me of, high up on the Comeragh Mountains and spread Pete's ashes by myself. I was of course worried that going solo was a bad idea. I was scared that I might have a breakdown while up there and be unable to make my way home. It wasn't like I had spread anyone's ashes before. I really didn't know how I would react.

When I shared this dilemma with my counsellor, she suggested that I make a quick video while up there, one only for my sons' eyes. They were still too small to accompany me up the mountain and too young to understand the ins and outs of cremation. My counsellor said that, if I captured the moment on film, it would be something they could look at when they got older and were able to understand more. At least then I would feel like my own family were there with me, as I faced the camera and spoke to the future versions of my boys.

Despite it being the end of May, the summer was refusing to materialise. Outside I could see the weather was dank and windy, with rain clouds threatening above the ridge. I decided to bring a large rucksack with me, with a couple of extra layers. Once at the site, I figured I'd be hanging around for a while and knew I would quickly feel the cold.

The rucksack was also large enough to hold Pete's ashes. I'm not sure if the amount of ash that normally comes back from crematoria equates directly to how large that person was, but with Pete coming in at six foot tall, there seemed to be a lot of ash in the box we received. Some had already been siphoned off so that Aran and Cahal could have small urns as keepsakes. A box of ashes had also been placed in the family's grave. Though Pete had never wanted to be buried, it seemed the right thing to do. It meant his elderly parents had a focal point that they could visit to remember their eldest son. His sister had placed some ashes in a heart-shaped necklace that she now wore. His brother had also visited a rugby pitch where Pete used to play and had gained permission to spread some ashes behind the posts.

Now I was on the final leg of letting Pete go free. I had pre-ordered two large cardboard tubes that would be light enough to transport up the hill. These I both filled to the brim, ready for Pete's final journey with me.

I drove to the car park east of The Gap as I'd done so many times before when going for a mountain run while visiting Pete's family. It all felt so surreal. I brought along a map of the Comeraghs, to keep an eye on the contours so that I could also claim the trip was a Quality Mountain Day for my Mountain Leader training log. No one had to know the real purpose of the mountain outing. All that was important was that I had done the trip and learned something from it.

I climbed towards The Gap, up the thick heathered slopes that covered the rutted blanket bog. I could feel the force of the wind exerting itself more and more as I continued my ascent. If I was hoping that Pete's ceremony would be calm and serene, a moment of bliss on the mountainside, all of these hopes were quickly blown away with the gathering storm.

After a momentary jog on the flattened col, I began the long, steep ascent northwest towards Knockanaffrin. With the strengthening winds, the ridge felt more exposed than ever. To my left, I could see the gentle slopes leading down towards the Nire Valley. To my right were the precipitous cliffs that housed many of the Comeraghs' infamous glacial lakes. Though I may have done so on a calmer day, I didn't dare pause to lean over the edge and take in the waters of Lough Coumdoula below.

Pete was never much of a mountain runner. His weak ankles had prevented him from ever getting into the sport. I thought it ironic that on his final journey I was giving him a piggyback, letting him mountain run with me. I hoped he was grateful for the lift.

As I ran along towards the Comeraghs' highest peak, I began to appreciate the fact that I had decided to run solo as part of this intimate ceremony. It was a good call. When I'm running in the mountains, they never let me dwell on the past, nor do they give me the space to worry about the future. When faced with life-threatening weather, death-defying cliffs and ankle-breaking terrain, my body and mind are often too preoccupied with self-preservation to think about anything else beyond the here and now. And right then, that was all I could cope with.

It meant I wasn't going over and over in my head how I would go about laying Pete's ashes, or how I would feel before, during or after such a ceremony. All I could think about at that moment was how I was feeling a bit cold and a little hungry. Without slowing, I pulled out my hat and gloves that I had stowed away in a side pocket. I also grabbed a cereal bar and munched on it as I climbed.

I had estimated that the journey itself would take around three hours: ninety minutes to climb to Pete's spot, maybe half an hour to do the deed, and then another sixty minutes for the downhill journey. I hadn't run for that length of time for quite a while, so I took it nice and easy, pulling myself back to conserve my reserves, walking on any uphills. I also didn't know how much I would expend emotionally when saying my goodbyes to Pete. I only had so much energy to give.

As I arrived at the raised area around Béal Muice, I took my time to find the right spot, checking that I could see the houses of Pete's loved ones below. I was glad that the mist had not descended that morning, as it so often does in those parts. All three buildings were clearly visible.

Pete's friend had also shared that he would sometimes go up there alone just to sit and think. I could see why he gravitated to such a place. It was like a safe haven of solitude, a place to get away from the hubris of noise in the pasturelands below, to see everything with a little more perspective.

Though I was high up on the ridge, small crags a couple of metres below me formed a natural shelter. I was glad to dip down into it, as the wind had picked up so much by now that I feared at times I would get blown over the edge. I placed my rucksack carefully on the ground, before opening it and quickly putting on my down jacket. The cold was already starting to bite as I pulled up my hood to try and keep some warmth. I then placed the cardboard containers holding Pete's ashes respectfully on the ground. Finally I extracted my phone from a waterproof stuff sack before sitting down to speak to my older boys.

As I started to record, I told them what I thought they would want to hear ten, twenty years from now. I told them the truth, the god's honest truth, because I had already learned that that was what was most helpful. All I remember from taking that film that day is seeing my face reflected back to me in the screen. I had never actually seen myself cry before, but there they were, tears tumbling down my face, one after the other, leaking out from a source that constantly refilled itself and breached its banks despite all my attempts to control it.

Feeling my hands going numb from the icy wind, I knew it was time to stop talking. Instead I propped the phone up on a tussock of grass facing outwards. Pressing the red button once more, I took a deep breath and unscrewed the top of the first container. By now the wind was blowing violently against my back, across the valley towards the untamed mountains where I stood, over the ridge towards the green homely farmlands below. Tipping the container ever so slightly, Pete's ashes immediately shot into the air. The rapidity of their disappearance startled me. It was like, despite my well-thought-out preparations, there wasn't even time for me to say my final farewells.

As I watched the dust plume rush out of my hands, it felt like Pete was desperate to be free; to be finally gone from every confine and inconvenience life had ever imposed on him. I also felt that, with the rapidity of his departure, he wanted to let me know that he no longer needed me.

Deep down, I knew it was the right thing to do, to let Pete go. He didn't need me anymore to nurse him through his illness, to stand by his side as his supportive partner. His final request, to be brought to the Comeragh Mountains, was it because he just needed me one last time, to carry him to a height? Only then would he have a high enough vantage point to be able to finally take flight?

Pete was always a mover and shaker when he was alive. At least now he no longer had to contend with airports or taxis or tuk-tuks or rickshaws to get around the globe. He'd be far happier now, I told myself, with the wind as his vehicle to carry him around the world.

I packed away my phone and the now empty cardboard containers before putting my rucksack back on. I had stayed still too long in my sweat-laden clothes. I was starting to feel the cold. I needed to get moving again to restore some semblance of warmth. The familiarity of running lulled away the enormity of what had just happened. I checked my map to confirm I was heading back in the right direction before running down the first slope.

My rucksack was lighter on the return journey, making the climb back up Knockanaffrin slightly easier. My legs were tired, however, and my heart was heavy. I staggered over boulder fields that lay in my path. I found myself struggling to traverse the shoe-sucking peat hags that I had bounded over an hour before. Even a sugary treat from my rucksack failed to revive. It wasn't long before I had to resign myself to the fact that I needed to sit down.

So there I was, slumped on the side of a mountain, feeling really shit. I'd never felt as drained as this on a simple half-day mountain run. I could feel the wetness of the cold dirt below me seeping through my clothes, chilling my skin. Despite this discomfort, I didn't want to move.

What was happening, unbeknownst to me, was that I was journeying backwards through the grief cycle. If anything restorative had happened over the past few months, this was slowly ebbing, and the numbness I felt on the day Pete died was making its return. It was only much later that I realised that the idea of a linear pathway through grief didn't work for me. Instead I bounced backwards and forwards between the supposed stages in a wildly random fashion.

I looked around at my surroundings, at The Gap stretching out below me and at Croughduff Mountain towering up above. There was no one out there but me. It felt satisfying, the thought of just staying there forever, seeping back into the bog, becoming part of a mountain where I could come to no further harm. The mountains had always been my refuge. Maybe I had reached the stage where I should stay with them forever.

The only thing that made me get back up was the thought of my kids. I had left them with their aunt and had told them I'd be back by lunchtime at the latest. I knew it wasn't fair on any of them if I reneged on my commitment.

I struggled back to my feet to continue the long run downhill back to my car. Normally I would have skipped and jumped and enjoyed every minute of letting gravity take its course. Instead each foot smacked against the ground, each shoe sunk into the brown mud, making me slide and stumble and fall.

It would take me a long time before I could process what happened that day. At the time, the departure of Pete's ashes at such high speed on that mountaintop had left me feeling bereft. Believing that it was a sign that he no longer needed me made me question so much. It was only much later that I could read into it slightly differently.

I've slowly come to terms with the possibility that Pete maybe wanted to be out of there fast so as to leave me the space to restart my own life. Maybe he wanted to tell me that, it wasn't he who didn't need me, but it was I who no longer needed him. They say if you love someone, let them go. Was that what we were doing to each other?

And just as I felt like I was left with a quarter glass of milk after Pete's death, maybe instead of focusing on the three-quarters that was spilt, I needed to see the opportunities in now having space within my container. Maybe, instead of milk I could add some ice-cream and chocolate sauce and make myself a milkshake? I was only forty-three, potentially only half-ways through my life. What other things, what other opportunities lay in-store instead?

As I journeyed back to my children, to relieve their aunt from babysitting, I was very, very far however from this interpretation of where my life was potentially headed. I was back to ground-zero and had to start again the long and arduous healing process.

CHAPTER 20

FOR ME

'**S**o how have you been doing?' my counsellor asked as we sat down opposite each other across my kitchen table. Her hands nursed a cup of tea I had just brewed for her. I hesitated, my brain struggling to find the right words to answer her simple question.

'Em, well,' I said, taking a deep breath. 'I suppose…well what I can say is…perhaps the main news is that I spread Pete's ashes last week…like I said I would.'

'And how did that go?' she asked, kindness in her tone.

I had to stop and think. I weighed my words carefully before finally letting them out.

'Fine, I think,' I replied. 'Like, not fine, but I…well, what I mean is. It's done now.'

She sat there, letting me stew in the silence that was of my own creating. I in turn stared at the mug in her hand that she had barely drunk from. She had a habit of always leaving cold tea behind her after she called at my house. She probably only accepted the drink out of politeness. I made a mental note not to offer her any more hot refreshments during our monthly meet-ups.

'Well, I guess,' I eventually continued. 'I suppose I'm not doing so well.'

This was the first time she had seen me this bad, my normal fluency gone, replaced with an inability to string words together to form coherent sentences. It was like I was in shock again, my brain shutting down to protect me from whatever it deemed the latest threat. She'd seen me sad before, but at least I'd always had some sort of redeeming feature; the kids were doing well all things considered; I'd secured better childcare arrangements for Cahal so that I could have more hours to work; I'd enrolled Aran into Scouts so that he'd have some good male role models around him. I was still doing stuff to make things better.

'I'm glad I caught you like this,' she said finally. 'It's really important you acknowledge your feelings at this stage.'

I had no issue with the concept of accepting my feelings. Every grief website I'd been on had given me this exact same piece of advice. It was only that, right then, I didn't have any feelings to feel. Numbness had truly embedded itself deep inside of me, cutting me off and casting me adrift from any sort of emotion.

I just sat there and prayed she wasn't going to suggest I join a local grief support group. I couldn't bear the idea of sitting in a room with others to talk about our respective losses. Just like I didn't want to do Cairnuary, to go up and down Slieve Martin for the month of January in remembrance of Pete, I instinctively knew that such a group activity just didn't fit right with me at that moment. I had to move forward, for the sake of the boys, not rehash the past. There would be plenty of time to do such reflection later.

'Can I ask, are you doing anything for yourself?' she continued, her head cocked gently to the side. I stared back at her blankly. 'I hear you saying that you're minding the boys, that they're your priority.' I nodded back in agreement. 'It just seems to me like you're minding everyone but yourself.' I felt myself deflate. Was I now going to fail at my counselling sessions when I had thus far performed so well?

Anyhow, I wasn't even sure what doing 'anything for myself' meant these days. Like I wasn't the type of person who needed to buy herself a new handbag or go for a spa day. Even the idea of going for a coffee with someone seemed an exhausting prospect. Though I knew quite early on that I needed to mind myself so that I could be of use to the boys, I thought that just meant that I had to make sure I slept, ate, exercised and basically kept functioning. Anything more luxurious than that was off the cards.

As she left me to deal with her cold tea, I filed away her admonishment to give it some further thought. The only thing I could think of that could give me any sense of satisfaction was going back mountain running. Despite the train wreck of a run that was my outing to scatter Pete's ashes, I had still enjoyed being out there in the dramatic and wild Comeraghs. Even though my training mojo was at an all-time low, I felt a hankering to be fit again to be able to do a long mountain run.

It was around this same time, as I wondered how I was meant to 'do something for myself', that I heard about Irish man, former Cork hurler and mountain runner Paul Tierney's ambitions to try and set a new Wainright record. The Wainwrights are an infamous list of 214 fells or mountains located within the UK's Lake District. These summits were diligently recorded within Alfred Wainwright's seven-volume *Pictorial Guide to the Lakeland Fells* published in the 1950s and sixties. The guide has since served many a hill walker as a tick list of mountains to climb, typically bagged over a couple of years.

In 2014, international orienteer Steve Birkenshaw set a mind-boggling time of six days, twelve hours and fifty-eight minutes to visit every single one of them, starting and finishing from the village of Keswick. In doing so, Steve covered 328 miles (about 527 kilometres) and climbed 36,000 metres in height, the equivalent of ascending Mount Everest four times from sea level. I had read Steve's book, *There's no Map in Hell*, an apt title for an ultra mountain-running feat that involved a lot of pain. Five years on, Paul Tierney was hoping to repeat the feat, only in a faster time.

Such ultra-running endeavours in the mountains have always intrigued me, so I was curious to see how Paul would do. But what made the attempt even closer to home was the fact that Paul was dedicating his run to his good friend and fellow endurance athlete, Chris Stirling, who had recently died tragically at the age of thirty-seven.

I watched Paul's Wainwright attempt unfurl throughout that week in June thanks to the power of social media and live online GPS tracking. I saw him run through the formidable Lakeland fells, with stupendous views surrounding him. I watched as he journeyed day and night with his friends, some of them household names within mountain-running circles, as they supported him in his endeavour. And as Paul arrived back in Keswick village, six days, six hours and five minutes later, he did so wearing his friend Chris's club vest. Paul had not only broken Steve's record by almost seven hours, but he also raised over £36,000 for the mental health charity, MIND.

Though Paul's mountain-running feat spoke to me on so many levels, Shelli Gordon's did so even more. Like me, Shelli had suffered the loss of a partner through suicide, a couple of months before I endured the exact same shock. She had seen no warning signs, however, no indication that Tony was unwell. She struggled to understand how someone like Tony, a successful runner and business owner, someone who seemingly had it all, could feel compelled to take their own life.

Shelli's grief spurred her on to run The Spine, a 268-mile non-stop race along the UK's Pennine Way (over 430 kilometres). Taking place in mid-January, The Spine strikes fear in the hearts of most endurance runners. In addition to the sheer scale of the event, it is renowned for its brutal conditions, with participants often having to contend with deep snow, ice, gale-force winds and torrential rain. Shelli battled on despite multiple injuries, a chest infection and borderline hypothermia during those five days and nights, securing second place in 128 hours and 26 minutes. She had originally set out to raise awareness of the extent of male suicide within our society and to raise a modest target of £1,400 for the mental health charity CALM. Her story spoke to so many that in the end she collected over £36,000.

What was probably most devastating about Paul and Shelli's stories was how even members of the running community couldn't escape the devastation that mental illness and suicide wreaks. The loved ones they dedicated their runs to, Chris and Tony, had both been physically fit and healthy, competing at the highest levels within the sport.

Thus far, I didn't know of any athletes who had directly suffered from mental health issues. I had somehow convinced myself that as a community we were pretty immune or that, if we were afflicted, mountain running allowed us to stay on top of our condition.

Though what Paul and Shelli accomplished was inspiring, I had no intention of emulating them by running for days on end. Firstly I knew it wouldn't be fair on the kids or their child minders. But more importantly, I had enough experience to realise how wrecked I'd be after being on my feet for that long. I would barely function. Anything I did had to allow me to come home afterwards and still be able to look after my three- and five-year-old.

I felt, however, the need to do some sort of event as opposed to just get fit again. I needed a goal to work towards, especially when training would inevitably become a slog.

I've always had a soft spot for the mountain rounds. I had done the Wicklow Round in May 2009 and then in May 2018, seven months before Pete died, before he even got sick, I had completed the Denis Rankin Round in Northern Ireland. My love for the mountain rounds was probably the reason my conversation with Jonny Muir on our Pentlands run had gravitated to these challenges. I had always hoped to one day do the UK mainland rounds, namely the Bob Graham in England, the Paddy Buckley in Wales and the Charlie Ramsay in Scotland, two of which Jonny had completed. Preparing and travelling across the Irish Sea to do one of these rounds was, however, a stretch too far at this stage.

Which brought me back to the Round that was literally in my own back yard. The Denis Rankin Round was started in 2014 after the tragic death of mountain-running pioneer Denis Rankin the year before during a fell race on Slievemoughanmore. Based in the Mourne Mountains, the Round takes in thirty-nine summits, covering a distance of around ninety kilometres with 6,200 metres of ascent, depending on which way you travelled. I had already tackled it on my own on a beautifully dry and warm summer's day, with Pete supporting me at some of the road crossings. Though I struggled with dehydration and horrible blisters, I had managed to complete it in twenty-one hours and twenty-four minutes.

Rounds are normally attempted during the summer months, for a host of very good reasons. There is more daylight on offer, making it easier to run. On the day I attempted, I could see clearly from 4.30 am right up until 11 pm. Even when it did get dark, I had the benefit of a full moon. The other advantage of summer running is the greater potential for good weather. Though my attempt day was a little too warm, you can luck out with cool, dry conditions that are perfect for just jogging along. The logic goes that the intimidating distance, terrain and climb is enough to contend with on a round without also battling darkness and cold.

And that is why a 'winter round' is something that is seen on an altogether different scale. This is a round that is completed on any day from the first of December through to the last day of February. Though of course weather can be fortuitously mild at that time of year, in general it involves a challenge that is a lot colder, a lot darker, and a lot wetter underfoot. Snow might also be involved.

Up until that stage, no woman had done a winter round on the island of Ireland, north or south. There was probably a good reason why. Despite this, I wondered if doing a winter Denis Rankin Round could be considered as 'doing something for myself'. To me, it was something as frivolous as drinking coffee with friends. There wasn't any real purpose to it really. I wondered if it would tick my counsellor's box.

As soon as I started thinking about a winter Denis Rankin Round, I could see another benefit of doing it. I had been wondering how I would mark Pete's first anniversary. I didn't want to attend yet another ceremony that failed to move me. I was also dreading being in the house, fearful I would replay that day, scene by scene, in my memory. If after the scattering of his ashes I could go back to square one, I could just as easily return to ground zero, or even worse, one year on from his passing.

Maybe, I began to think, I could use a winter Denis Rankin Round to remember Pete's life and death around his anniversary? Maybe that would be my way of celebrating him instead of being sucked back down into the vortex of never-ending sadness?

The other thing that was important to me was that, whatever I did, it had to be low stress. Though I was truly amazed by the fundraising efforts of Paul and Shelli, I knew undertaking such a money-raising drive would totally stress me out, even if it was for a worthwhile cause. I just wanted to do a long run, without any hype or ceremony.

I was under no illusions about how difficult a winter round would be. So many things could go wrong, and if they did circumstances could deteriorate rapidly. So, unlike the summer rounds, which I'd done alone, I decided that I wasn't willing to risk a winter solo round.

It wasn't hard to think of someone who would be willing and able to accompany me. If my mate Paul Mahon could save me from the perils of getting stuck on Cove cliffs during the Mourne Mountain Marathon, then he'd be the right person to run with during a winter round.

I resolved to float the idea past him the next time I saw him. The opportunity arose a couple of weeks after I had set Pete's ashes free, on a warm summer July's day. I was down in Wicklow doing some quality mountain days for my Mountain Leader logbook. After a pleasant spell on the hills I called into Paul's place, a cosy pad in Wicklow's Glenmalure Valley.

'So are you ready to get racing again?' Paul asked me as soon as I was in the door.

'Paul, will you give it a break, will ye?' I replied, half-joking as I threw my rucksack down. 'I've told you, I'm not racing this year.' I knew Paul's question was well intentioned. He didn't want me to disappear into a deep, dark hole of depression, yet his enthusiasm was slightly premature, at times a tad overwhelming. I knew him well enough, however, to realise how to channel his puppy energy. 'I've a different idea, if you're interested,' I continued. 'How about doing a winter Denis Rankin Round with me?'

Paul didn't hesitate for a second. 'Sure,' he said. 'Great idea.'

'I was thinking of doing it in memory of Pete,' I went on to explain. 'I just thought it'd be a powerful statement, to run in the dark to remember what he went through.'

Running in darkness to support those bereaved by suicide is not a new concept in Ireland. Since 2009, the Darkness into Light movement has held events all around the country. Starting just before dawn, people run or walk a five-kilometre course, crossing the finish line just as the sun starts to rise. Not only has Darkness into Light raised over 25 million euro, with the concept spreading to fifteen other countries in the process, but they have helped form a strong community dedicated to breaking the stigma and destroying the prevalence of self-harm and suicide. What I was hoping to do, a ninety-kilometre mountain run, could have been considered as the equivalent of Darkness into Light, albeit on steroids.

The reason I had asked Paul was not just because of his mountain-running prowess. Paul had also been Pete's friend. I had confided in Paul at a race start back in August that Pete had not been well, when I broke down in tears just before registration. So concerned had Paul been that he actually visited us in our home just before Christmas, a few days before Pete died. He was struggling with the fact that, at Pete's time of need, he couldn't have helped more. Paul too was going through his own grieving process. He was happy to help me with mine.

'So when you thinking of doing it?' Paul asked me. 'Just need to make sure I'm fit enough by then!' I explained how we had a three-month window for it to qualify as a winter round. It all depended on getting suitable weather. If the weather was right on Pete's anniversary at the end of December, all well and good. Delaying, however, to late January or February would get us a sliver more daylight. We'd just have to keep an eye on the forecasts and make the date call closer to the time.

'But I just wanted to say,' I continued, 'I don't mind if we don't make it under the twenty-four hours.' For the round to be officially recognised, for your names to appear on the Denis Rankin Round membership list, the time recorded needed to be less than a day. Paul and I were already on the list from our respective summer rounds. In normal circumstances, one mention was quite enough. 'I just don't want the pressure of a ticking clock in case something goes wrong,' I explained. 'Let's just go out and do the course and enjoy it, if possible.'

Paul was happy enough to go with my suggestion for a low-stress winter jog in the Mourne Mountains, no matter how long it took us.

If Pete had a say, he probably would have wondered why I wanted to do something so hard and scary. He always thought I had a crazy streak. But once out there, I know Pete would have been the first to cheer me on at the road stops, to stand there clapping madly at the finish line. Doing this would have made him infinitely proud of me.

CHAPTER 21

BACK TRAINING

With Paul on board, the next person I had to speak to was my coach, Eamonn. As soon as I explained to him what I was thinking, he was all on for the idea. His steadfast support, not just in terms of coaching, meant a lot to me during that difficult, uncertain time.

Up until then, Eamonn had been giving me short daily sessions to keep me ticking over. They had kept me fit enough to be able to go out on hikes and runs as part of my business. The most I was ever out on my feet was three hours, and that was with lots of stopping and starting to check out maps and views. There was nothing too strenuous involved. There was no way that my level of fitness was enough to do twenty-four hours non-stop. Whether I liked it or not, I had to start doing some proper, consistent training if I wanted to be able to do a winter Denis Rankin Round.

After much poring over my schedule, I realised the only time I could really knuckle down and train properly was from August onwards. With a potential winter round in late December or January, that would give me around five months to get fit again. It was just about do-able.

The reason August was the best time to restart my training regime was that Aran, Cahal and I were heading off at that time on holidays with Dervla Campervan. Earlier in the year, I had made a pledge that I would carve out a chunk of time to spend with my boys during their summer break. On our return from our successful one-week Easter break in Scotland, I had booked us a three-week summer stay in France in campsites around Brittany and La Vendée. I thought it would be a good chance to have some quality family time.

My campsite choice was limited to those that had kids' clubs. With no Pete around, I had to have some sort of childcare every day so that I could go off for a run or bike. Without a kids' club I'd be forced to look after Aran and Cahal 24/7. Even I had to admit that there was only so much quality family time I could take.

Our vacation got off to a great start with the overnight ferry from Rosslare to Cherbourg. Aran and Cahal were super psyched with the idea of sleeping in cabin bunk beds on an actual boat. The excitement didn't stop there. There was even a kids' area on board where they could hang out and play. I stationed myself close to the playroom to make sure I looked like a responsible parent.

When planning the trip, it hadn't occurred to me that my single-parent status would stick out like a sore thumb. All the other children who were frolicking around had a mummy and daddy in tow. Maybe only nuclear families were supposed to go on holiday? I'd obviously missed that memo. I sat at my table, feeling a little sorry for myself. It wasn't until I heard Aran and Cahal chatting with some other kids that I told myself to chill. The fact that they only had one parent didn't seem to bother them. I looked over to see them kneeling together snugly with their newfound friends around a child-sized table, doing some colouring-in that the ferry's animators had provided.

'Power Rangers are awesome,' I overheard Aran saying to a brand-new chum.

'I like Pokemon,' the young boy replied without even looking up from his scribbling.

I could see Cahal watching them both, listening intently to this big boys' conversation.

'Yeah, but our daddy died,' Cahal shouting it out loud, so all could hear him. At that moment I wanted a massive fissure to open up in the ocean's floor, and for the ferry and I to be swallowed whole.

I stared straight ahead to avoid any surreptitious sideways glances from nearby couples that may have overheard. I couldn't bear the idea of adult eye contact. While I wondered if I should head over and do some impromptu counselling for the poor unfortunate boy, I saw Aran, Cahal and their new friend still actively colouring, none of them having even batted an eyelid. Finally the boy spoke.

'I like Power Rangers too,' he said in response to the death announcement, as if Cahal's statement about his father's demise was the most natural thing in the world. If the kids thought it was okay to speak like that, and their friend didn't mind, maybe I too needed to relax a little about our family situation.

We docked safely in Cherbourg the next day. It was a short drive to our first campsite, a drive that would have been made infinitely easier if our in-van GPS actually had a map of France installed, a fact I'd not checked before leaving Ireland. It would also have helped if vehicles on the continent didn't drive on the other side of the road, my right-hand drive making things even trickier. My stress levels kept on finding good reasons to edge ever upwards.

Even when we arrived at the campsite and found our pitch, things got no better. I soon saw how inexperienced we were as campers. While I was happy to just pop our top and be done with our set-up, I looked around to see all the paraphernalia I had forgotten. We had no barbeque set, no swing-tennis set-up, no gazebo. We hadn't brought fairy lights or flags or potted plants for pitch decoration. We were total amateurs.

I sat down inside our van and cracked open a bottle of wine to relieve the stress. At least I'd not forgotten to bring along some alcohol. I threw the white wine down my throat, hoping it would make me feel better. If anything, it made me feel ten times worse.

Pete and I had bought the campervan so that we could do exactly this; travel to France, hang out with the kids, drink cool white wine together. If he'd just waited, even for a couple of more months, then he could have come with us. If he'd just hung out a little longer, maybe he would have got better. I could feel anger bubbling up inside me, anger that had probably been there, fermenting all this time. Just when I thought that a holiday would be a time for me to relax and unwind, all it was doing was giving a space for me to experience the full wrath of my inner rage.

Fortunately there was enough entertainment around the place for the boys to not notice my plight. There were swimming pools and playgrounds and outdoor pony rides. There was mini-golf and a zip-line and a bouncy castle. They flitted from one thing to the next, totally high with excitement.

Even the daily kids' club was perfect for them. The animators seemed so extraordinarily happy to see my boys. They also were delirious to see the other twenty-odd kids who were being dumped there for the morning. They either loved kids or were exceptionally well trained. It made me feel a little less guilty about leaving them there with total strangers.

The first day I dropped them off, I had already donned my running gear. Eamonn had given me a seventy-minute run to do. No crazy efforts, no mad speed, just an easy gentle jog, he stipulated, for me to get back into the swing of things. I'd found out that there was a walkers' track leading out of the campsite that went on a ten-kilometre loop. It was perfect for the job.

I ran out of the campsite, trying to keep things nice and slow. I could already see from my watch's heart rate reading how unfit I was. The number emblazoned across its screen was way too high for my effort. It was to be expected. With time and consistent training, I knew the figure would come down. I had to start somewhere, however, if I wanted to get fit enough for a ninety-kilometre mountain run in five months' time.

The circuit proved to be exceptionally pleasant in the end. It snaked its way through a nearby cobblestoned village with the smell of freshly baked bread oozing from the local *boulangerie*. It brought me through dense woodland that shaded me from the growing daytime heat that we had come to France in search of. It led me past golfers on their cool greens, some of whom took time out from their intense competition to shout words of encouragement.

I woke up the next morning practically crippled. I could barely bum-shuffle my way out from our roof-top bed. My quads screamed blue murder when I tried to sit down. Forget my heart rate data. My legs were in no way up for an ultra-mountain run if I could barely manage a gentle seventy-minute jog along flat forest trails. It was depressing. If I had just wanted to get fit again, I'd have struggled to stick to the training timetable Eamonn had given me. But because I had a goal, something particular I wanted to do, I gritted my teeth as I pulled up that day's schedule and just got on with it.

As the days passed, Aran, Cahal and I slowly got into a holiday routine. Our days began with *pain au chocolat*, with coffee for me, before heading to the local shop to buy some fresh baguettes. I'd get my training done in the morning while Aran and Cahal were at kids' club. Afterwards we'd head to the swimming pool where my boys would splash around, while I'd devour the next book on my Kindle.

If everyone had been good, we'd head back to the local shop to buy some ice-cream. Back at Dervla Campervan, we'd unwrap our lollies and sit quietly, slurping up our holiday treat. The simplicity of it all was disarming. That's probably why, during one particular ice-cream session, I got the shock of my life. Aran was in mid-lick as he turned and asked me, 'How did Daddy die?' I choked on a chocolate waffle bit.

All my bereavement books were on a bookshelf back home. I had packed no go-to guides with me that explained how to answer this question in an age-appropriate manner. I was acutely aware one of my sons would ask it eventually. I just hadn't anticipated it while we were on holiday.

I hide my silence in my ice-cream eating as I tried to formulate a response in my head. I was also hoping something else edible would distract Aran and make him forget he'd enquired in the first place.

'So how did he die then?' Aran asked again when I hadn't replied within his allotted timeframe. There is no point avoiding it any longer, I thought. I might as well tell them now.

'Well, people can die in three main ways,' I said, diving into my first-aid training that had formed part of my Mountain Leader award. 'They call it ABC. Airways, Breathing, Circulation.' Aran looked at me intensely. I regretted having captured so successfully his undivided attention. 'So their airways can get blocked, that's A, or they can stop breathing, which is B, or their blood can stop going round and round, which is C for circulation.' I looked back at Aran to see if he was following me. 'Well your Daddy,' I said, coughing slightly to clear my throat before announcing the inevitable. 'It was his breathing. It was B. He stopped breathing.' And with this admission, I felt a single tear commence the slow descent of my cheek. Counting off the days since my last teary moment, I hadn't cried in weeks. I now had to reset the counter to zero thanks to this conversation.

'Why are you crying, Mummy?' Aran said, unaware of the effort this explanation had taken out of me.

'I suppose I miss Daddy,' I said, as I failed to stop another tear from escaping.

'I miss Daddy too,' Aran replied.

'Me too,' Cahal said, chiming in at the end so solemnly despite the ridiculous clown face of melted ice-cream plastered all around his mouth.

I sat there, feeling miserable, wondering if I had just ruined our holiday.

'Can we go to the bouncy castle now?' Aran then asked, throwing me a lifeline. I had given him sufficient information, and he was content to run with that.

'Me too!' Cahal shouted back, bouncing up and down in his chair. And with that unexpected change in conversation topic, the cause of their daddy's death was laid to rest for a little while.

I continued to put in my daily training while we holidayed in France. One of the advantages of travelling with Dervla Campervan was that, not only was I able to bring my bike, but there was also plenty of space in our vehicle to bring my rollers as well. I had taken them along in case I couldn't find any suitable roads to ride on. Once in France, seeing that I was the only adult in our party and so didn't want to risk anything happening me, I decided to make full use of them. So, once the boys were dropped to kids' club, I'd return to Dervla, set up my rollers beside her back door and ride my bike for an hour or two. It must have looked silly to the other campers, to be using my holiday time to effectively ride absolutely nowhere, but I was at a stage where I was resigned to do whatever I had to do and not to worry what others thought.

Despite taking precautions to ensure I didn't have a road accident, it didn't stop me from falling sick during our break. One day I woke up in the van and felt horribly unwell. It was just a cold, but it still knocked me for six.

'Go play with your laptops,' I begged the boys as soon as they woke up. 'Mummy needs just to lie down for a while.' Aran and Cahal were more than happy to oblige as they nipped to their seats and fired up their screens. I lay there in bed, feeling sorry for myself. My body ached all over and my kidneys felt incredibly sore.

It's at times like this that you realise the pressure of single parenting. If anything happened me, the boys were scuppered. Even getting unwell for a day put the total skids on their holiday. Absolutely everything depended on me.

I remembered how in his final days I had begged with Pete to think of our kids, to just be there for them, to do whatever the medical professionals told him so that he could get better.

'They want you here physically,' I had implored. 'They don't care if you're not here mentally.'

'It's not enough,' was Pete's sorrowful reply. How wrong he had been. His physical presence was missed immensely, was so acutely needed on so many levels. Depression tells its victim so many convincing lies, with so many unfortunate consequences.

Being away on holiday with just the two boys allowed other things to come to light as well. When at home, I'd always bump into someone I knew when out and about, at the school gates, the local park or in the village shops. There'd always be a five-minute conversation with someone, a chance to shoot the breeze. Sometimes those brief interactions also allowed me to get off my chest something small that was getting me down that day, defusing it before it turned into a massive deal.

Now that I was on holiday, I didn't have the chance to have such mini check-ins. Sending a text or WhatsApp message back home proved too much hassle. Instead, when a thought came to mind that caused me concern, I wasn't randomly bumping into a friend who would tell me not to worry. While on holiday, snowflake thoughts and anxieties snowballed. In the absence of familiar faces, I fended off these emotional avalanches by drinking more and more. I figured I was on holiday, it didn't matter, but deep down I knew it wasn't good. I resigned myself to getting through the holiday with a topped-up wine glass in hand, albeit with a renewed appreciation of the support network back home that was helping me through my loss.

In the final days of our vacation, I tried to make the most of our French stint for the sake of my sons. Aran proved brave enough to taste a pot of *moules frites* that I'd ordered at a restaurant. Friendly neighbours invited the boys to their adjoining site to learn the art of *pétanque*. Then when we were hanging out at the pool one day, a French girl around ten years old tried to converse with Aran.

'Mummy, Mummy,' Aran said, getting out of the pool to get my attention. 'What is that girl saying to me?'

The girl followed Aran out of the waters and approached me.

'*Comment s'appelle ton fils?*' she asked, pointing to my son who was returning to the pool. Dragging my French vocabulary from the recesses of my brain, I told her his name was Aran.

'Ah-ran, Ah-ran!' she shouted as she dived back into the water after him. Aran had just turned six, way too young to be a love interest for this admittedly very pretty girl. But somehow she had taken a real shine to my boy, and wanted to spend time with him.

We continued to bump into her around the campsite, and she always seemed so happy to see her new friend. It may have been because it was a chance for her to practise speaking English, but generally they seemed to just enjoy playing together.

I couldn't help watching Aran with his much older blonde French female friend and thinking how Pete would have been so proud of his son. Pete always said his boys would be a real catch for some lucky women.

I was also very proud of both of them, but not in that way. I was just proud to see them growing up and dealing so well with everything that had been thrown at them that year.

CHAPTER 22

TESTED

We arrived home from our French summer break just in time for Aran to go back to school and Cahal to start at the local nursery. I was relieved to get back to familiar places and faces and to kickstart again some sort of routine. While they were busy learning their ABCs and their 123s, I began my final preparations for my Mountain Leader award assessment.

The five-day examination was due to take place at the end of October. I had already fulfilled all the pre-requisites in terms of training courses and quality mountain days, so I spent the final few weeks leading up to it just brushing up on my skills. The one that needed most refining was my night navigation. I had already put in a considerable amount of mountain navigation practice during daylight hours but, when navigating at night, everything had to be spot on. Make one mistake and it was very easy to get disorientated and end up very, very lost.

Rachy was happy to accompany me for a bit of night navigation practice. We met up at Meelmore Lodge, to take in the boulder-strewn undulating area north of Slieve Meelmore. We caught up on news as we walked along the farm laneway leading towards the mountain. As soon as we hit the slopes, however, all conversation ended abruptly. The level of concentration we needed to ensure we didn't get lost in the dark meant that there was no room for idle chit-chat.

'Should we try and hit this sheep-pen?' Rachy said, shining her head-torch beam on a miniature box drawn on our maps. If it had been daytime, we could have looked up and proclaimed, 'There it is.' In the dark, however, we both knew it would take every bit of our brainpower to find that stone enclosure.

I stood stock still for a while to calculate my timing and pacing. When I was absolutely sure they were correct and that I had committed the numbers to memory, I stepped into the night.

'One, two, three, four...' I muttered under my breath so as not to disturb Rachy in her own navigational trance. I had to precisely count all my steps if I was going to find this abandoned former sheep shelter. At the same time I had to shine my head-torch diligently over the rough ground, to make sure I didn't land my foot awkwardly in some hidden hole masked by a heather clump. During the day, I wouldn't have needed to concentrate so much on foot placement. At night, however, everything was just so much harder to see, with consequences of getting it wrong so much more pronounced.

Rachy and I were pleased to see the sheep-pen come into focus with only a couple more seconds to go.

'Nice job,' I said, feeling immensely proud of ourselves. If I could repeat such a leg during the assessment, I would most likely pass.

When it came to a winter Denis Rankin Round, however, I was well aware that night navigation would be on a totally different scale. I wouldn't have the time to stand around and make those kinds of precise pacing and timing calculations if we wanted to get under the twenty-four hours. Granted, I only had to find prominent summits, not four by four meter sheep-pens, but accuracy was still key. My head also hurt a little after that five-minute leg. How could I possibly keep up such levels of concentration for what could potentially be fifteen hours of darkness, all going well?

It was at that time that I needed to remind myself of the purpose of my winter round attempt. I wasn't doing it as a feat of mountain-craft and running endurance. It wasn't something I was doing to challenge myself personally. My reason for tackling the route in mid-winter was to remember my husband. It didn't really matter if I slowed down or made mistakes, and yet, if there was anything I could do to make the route-finding aspect of the winter round any easier, I was willing to accept it.

While the mountain-running community had been busy that year determining which races did not allow GPS usage, the Denis Rankin Round committee had already decided long before that GPS was allowed during round attempts. In doing so they were following in the footsteps of the other UK rounds where GPS is permitted. Only Ireland's Wicklow Round south of the border had expressly banned such electronic gadgetry for navigational or pacing assistance.

Knowing how hard night navigation is with just map and compass, I opted to relax my purist principles for once. I decided that, seeing that it was allowed, I was going to go ahead and use a GPS when running a winter Denis Rankin Round. In my book, the distance, cold, darkness and possible outbursts of grief were enough to contend with. What also eased my decision was that, if something did go wrong, if Paul and I experienced GPS failure while out there, I still had the knowledge, skills and confidence to get us home under the pure steam of map and compass.

As I continued to ponder on how best to go about doing a winter round, my thoughts gravitated to the people who had been so supportive both

on and off the mountains during the previous year. I remembered mountain runners who had called at my house to offer me their condolences. I
thought of clients who weren't afraid to approach me after a course and ask
me how things were going. I thought of orienteers who had kindly offered
to mind Aran and Cahal so I could amble around courses. There was part
of me that wanted to share my remembrance run with them, to thank them
for everything they'd done.

The Denis Rankin Round, again like the UK rounds, allows support
while on the hills. You can have accompanying runners who navigate for
you, carry your gear or even just provide entertainment to distract you
from the pain. They are allowed to start and stop along the route whenever,
wherever they like.

The Wicklow Round, which I completed in 2009, doesn't allow such
supporters or pacers. If you start solo, you stay solo. If you're in a group,
no one can join in halfway. In keeping with this rule, I had done a solo
Wicklow Round, and when I attempted the Denis Rankin Round nearly a
decade later, I opted to repeat my solo strategy and enjoy a nice summer's
day on the hills on my own.

But this time, it was different. My priorities had changed. What if I
invited others to run with Paul and me for sections of a winter round? It
would be a chance to meet up with fellow orienteers, mountain runners and
friends who I'd not seen in a while because of my racing break. It would
also be great if others could navigate for us, carry some safety equipment
for us, engage us in random conversations to help the time pass. It would
make things less arduous.

With four months to go, I kept this final thought to myself. I had only
spoken to Paul and Eamonn thus far about the plan. If I came to my senses

at any point, I wanted to be able to quietly back out without the mountain community any wiser. If I started asking people to sign up for stages, it meant that I was committed to doing a winter round. It would permit them to check in on me, to see how my training was going, to hear how my plan was progressing. I still had doubts about whether I would even do it, whether I would be fit enough in time. I also wasn't sure how I'd cope with Pete's first anniversary, whether it would send me tumbling backwards again.

We returned from France in September, the month that also marked what would have been Pete's fiftieth birthday. I wasn't sure how I would react come the day. Not only was it the first time I would live through his birthday without him, but it was also such a significant age. You only turn fifty once. But when the date arrived, it turned out to be a day like any other. I didn't descend into the depressive state I thought I would.

It was probably because Pete hated his birthdays, didn't like cards or presents or parties. I knew him well enough to know that he would have probably just wanted a glass of wine on the couch in front of the nine o'clock news to mark the occasion, maybe a slice of cake at most. It wouldn't have been a big deal for him, so it wasn't an issue for me either. His friends and family, however, reacted differently. They would have celebrated, thrown a surprise party, would have made a big fuss. The date of his birth shook them when they considered what could have been.

What affected me much more than his birthday was living through our first wedding anniversary apart. I couldn't help but think of all the expectations I had that day all dressed in white, expectations that had been subsequently erased. I had assumed we'd have children who we'd watch grow up, and then see their own children, our grandchildren in turn. I thought of how I had presumed 'until death do we part' would occur when we were old and grey-haired and frail. The weight of dashed expectations came crashing down on top of me on our anniversary. How foolish I had been to think that we would have had a normal life where we'd grow old together.

While I was writhing from the despair of vows played out too soon, no one else was experiencing this pain. I was the only one who remembered our wedding day. How curious how some are profoundly affected by certain dates, while others are bowled over at another one entirely.

With all this personal drama playing out in the background, I continued to prepare for my Mountain Leader award assessment at the end of October. I checked my gear, then re-checked it, before checking it once more just in case. I re-read the books, studied the maps, and practised my emergency knots over and over at home. When the first day of assessment arrived, I knew there was no further preparation I could do. Whatever happened out there happened. I was as ready as I could be to give it my best shot.

Seven other candidates were put through their paces together with me. Three assessors joined us, one of whom had acted as a trainer on my original course. Their job was simple; to determine whether they would feel comfortable entrusting their own children to us on a journey through the mountains.

For the whole five days, we were marched up, down and around the Mourne Mountains, to many areas that I'd fortunately visited before. Our first day of navigation brought me to the place I'd been on my first day of mountain-leader training. Our second day of rope work and steep ground techniques were on Spellack, right where Rachy had had her emergency wedgie. And our three-day expedition started off close to my home village of Rostrevor, to parts of the mountain range that I'd hiked and run through many times before.

By the time we hiked off the mountain on the final day, descending on the tracks through Tollymore Forest towards the centre where we'd started, I felt extremely tired from the non-stop assessment pressure. I had also barely slept for the two nights of wild camping, which wasn't helped by our 2 am bedtime after testing our night navigation. Throughout those five days I had got some things right. I had also made silly mistakes. I wasn't sure though if on balance I'd performed well enough to make the grade.

We were all of course extremely relieved when our instructor announced to us on the walk back to the centre that we had all successfully passed. He also said if we wanted more detailed feedback, then we were welcome to stay on for a personal debrief session with the assessors. I opted to take them up on their offer.

Despite knowing the result, I still felt quite nervous as I stepped into the room to face my examiners. I shouldn't have worried as they said kind things, remarking on how far I'd come since stepping into the centre the previous year. I was no longer just a mountain runner. I was now a full-on mountain leader.

I hadn't intended to say anything except to thank them for their time. But when the moment came for me to speak, something inside me gave.

'I'm not sure if you know,' I said, 'But my husband died last year.' Two of the assessors nodded their heads, while one hadn't been made aware. 'I just wanted to thank you for letting me continue on with the training during that time, when you could have advised me to stop.' It must have been the tiredness that made me get emotional. 'Doing this Mountain Leader award has really helped me get through this time. And I just wanted to say thanks.' I hadn't cried in nearly two months, so I had plenty of tears stored up for when the perfect moment arose.

Some may have questioned whether I should have continued with the Mountain Leader award after Pete's sudden death. They could have assumed that I was throwing myself into such a large undertaking in order to avoid dealing with my grief. Such an assumption was entirely understandable.

Except that, to the contrary, the Mountain Leader award gave me something positive to focus on when everything else around me was so hard. It made me slow down to appreciate the mountains in a way I'd not done before. It also introduced me to new people, allowing me to help those who wanted to learn more, as well as giving me the space to become friends with those who love the mountains just as much as I.

As I stood up to leave, one assessor gave me a big hug. They all wished me well with my new endeavours, with an assurance that I'd probably bump into them again when I was out and about on the hills.

Completing my Mountain Leader award made me feel like I'd fallen off a cliff. I had dedicated so much time and energy to it that, when it was over, it quickly became apparent that I'd nothing lined up in its place to distract myself with. Come November, business was also slack. The racing season was over and the winter weather was fast approaching. People weren't interested anymore in heading out in the hills to learn how to navigate. I quickly became bored and needed to fill the gap. I was also anxious that inactivity might not be good for my mental state in the run up to Pete's first anniversary.

I was still bumbling along with training for a winter Denis Rankin Round. With only two months left until a potential attempt, if I was going to enlist the help of a team of supporters, I needed to commit. People would soon be turning to their 2020 diaries and filling up weekends with

TESTED

events, unbeknownst to them that a global pandemic was just around the corner, waiting to throw their race schedules into turmoil.

After much thought, I decided to reach out to the orienteering community. Many of them were also mountain runners, people who knew the Mournes extremely well. Orienteers are also notorious for being super reliable. If you tell them where you want them, when you want them, they never fail to turn up in the right place right on time. The easiest way to gauge interest was to post on my local orienteering club's group chat.

I told them I wanted to do something to mark one year on from my late husband Pete's passing, something that had meaning. I said that after much thought, I had decided to try and do a winter Denis Rankin Round in the coming months.

'There is something about running in the dark with a group of friends in formidable mountains that sends out a strong message,' I wrote. 'It reminds us to mind our own health as well as to look out for each other,' I added, after some thought. I told them that I wasn't going to fundraise like Paul Tierney or Shelli Gordon had. Instead I was inviting people to join me on stages of the round, to run for a while in the cold and dark.

Within minutes of me posting this message, stalwart orienteer and mountain runner Sharon Dickenson replied.

'Count me in,' she said. Within seconds Sharon added that sprint-orienteer specialist Susan Lambe, who happened to be sitting beside her right at that moment, was available to meet us at road crossing points for us to restock supplies. It wasn't long before Sharon also had mountain runner Niall Gibney, the first person to complete a winter Denis Rankin Round, on board. It seemed like Sharon had an uncanny knack of convincing others to sign up for round duties. I made a mental note of her persuasive abilities,

223

figuring that they would come in handy at a later stage.

Before I knew it, a raft of other orienteers and mountain runners had freely committed to assist Paul and me on our winter round attempt. I saw Billy Reed, one of the first people to complete the Denis Rankin Round as well as a Barkley Marathons starter, offer up his services. Experienced mountain runner, Kathleen Monteverde, who had recently chalked off her own solo Denis Rankin Round signed up quickly too. There was Liam Smyth, a member of the Mourne Mountain Rescue Team, saying he was more than happy to help. The breadth and depth of support offered so quickly was truly overwhelming.

Having a long list of benevolent and experienced helpers both on and off the hills meant that, even if I wanted to, I couldn't back out now. Whether I liked it or not, I has no choice but to give a winter Denis Rankin Round a go.

CHAPTER 23

RECCES

The Denis Rankin Round is roughly divided into five stages, with road or major track crossings at the end of each section acting as natural breaks. Given that runners can start at whatever time of day or night they like, it was totally up to Paul and me which stages we'd like to tackle in the dark and to determine which ones would be best done in daylight.

The easiest part to do at night time is that from Loughshannagh Mountain to the finish in the seaside town of Newcastle. This is because the majority of this stretch involves blindly following the massive, couldn't-miss-it-if-you-tried Mourne wall. If I was going to learn how to use a GPS, this would be the most convenient section to teach myself on. If anything went wrong, I'd still have a seven-foot wall right beside me to tell me where to go.

Despite the reassurance of having such technology with me, I didn't want to do the section on my own. Like my young kids, I was still afraid of monsters that came out at night that might chase after me across mountaintops, catch me, and then eat me all up in one bite. So I enlisted the help of mountain runner and GP Áine McNeill and previous Maurice Mullins Ultra winner Denise Mathers, two ladies who were preparing for their own attempt on the Denis Rankin Round within the coming year. They brought their friend, Karen, who'd just claimed the Causeway Coast Marathon title. I in turn dragged along my friend, Wiola Gorman, a recent finisher of the one hundred and seventy kilometre Ultra Trail de Mont Blanc (UTMB) race.

We might have been five women going for a run in in the pitch black in some of the highest mountains in Northern Ireland, but put together we were a feckin' awesome bunch of females that could probably conquer everything. It was just like Rachy, Cara and myself scaling the heights of Spellack together as part of our mountain-leader training; just a group of girls refusing to be told that we couldn't because of our gender.

Regardless of this formidable line-up, I was still petrified of going on the run. Dropping my kids off to Leona, my mountain-biking friend who had agreed to mind them, I couldn't help sharing my concern.

'I really don't want to go,' I said, standing in her hallway, delaying my departure as long as I possible.

'You'll have a great time,' she said. 'Sure I only wish I could join you.'

'Want to swap?' I said.

Leona laughed. I wasn't joking.

If I hadn't been meeting up with the other four, I'd have put Aran and Cahal back in my car and driven straight home. Subconsciously I knew it would be fine, that we'd have a good run out and that we'd get home safe, but standing on the cusp of it, all I felt was violently sick. Nerves had well and truly set in for the night.

'If I'm not back before 11pm, call Mountain Rescue,' I said, knowing I had reached the point of no return.

'Will you stop it? You'll be fine,' Leona said, pushing me out the front door. 'Have fun!'

Áine, Denise, Karen and Wiola were bouncing with excitement when I met up with them in Newcastle's Donard Park. We'd agreed to rendez-vous there, then drive one car to the start of stage five before running back to our vehicles via eight mountain peaks.

Perhaps it was the fact that I felt responsible for them that made me so nervous. I was the one who had organised the outing. I was the one holding the GPS. I was the qualified mountain leader in the group. If anything happened, I was the one who had to rescue us.

Or perhaps I was overthinking this.

My childminder Leona was right about our run being fun as we jogged up and over Ott Mountain before hitting the wall at the base of Loughshannagh. The sun was setting gently on this autumnal evening, and we had the whole of the Mourne Mountains to ourselves.

'That's so class,' Wiola said, gazing out over towards Doan and the gentle waters of Silent Valley Reservoir that were disappearing into the twilight. I barely broke stride as I glanced over to what she was seeing. I had to agree with Wiola. It was pretty class alright.

With the sun disappearing below the horizon as we strode up Slieve Meelbeg, I started to feel the pressure of having to night navigate. Much to my surprise, as I stared at my GPS, it knew exactly where we were and showed me precisely where we had been. And true to form, the wall was there as it promised to be. It directed us cleanly over Slieve Meelmore, Slieve Bearnagh, Slievenaglogh and Slieve Corragh without the slightest error.

Coming off the last mountain Slieve Commedagh was magical. Far below us, the welcoming glow of Newcastle lit up the sky that had thus far been devoid of light. We'd been on the mountain for less than three hours, never more than three kilometres away from civilisation, and yet it had felt like we had just journeyed to one of the remotest parts of the world.

Breaking through Donard forest, arriving back at sea level, we soon found ourselves exposed to the bright glare of car headlights. The infamous local boy racers were back in town, lining themselves up in Donard car park for their nightly spins of speed through the streets and out into the deserted countryside. Their engine revs deafened our ears that had gotten used to nothing but the sound of each other's laboured breaths out on the mountain slopes. Tooting horns soon added to these revs, as these boy racers saw a bunch of five lovely ladies jogging past their windscreens. I'm not sure if it was them or us who started the wolf whistling, but it was definitely us who were responsible for the manic giggling.

'That was fab. Let's do that again,' Wiola said as soon as we'd arrived at our vehicles. I realised a fifteen-kilometre mountain run was nothing compared to the one hundred and seventy alpine trail race she was used to, but I had had enough for one night.

'Have to relieve the childminder,' I said, making my excuses before driving home back across the mountain range.

My prudence at only running for three and a half hours that night was fortuitous. It turned out that going any further would have been ill advised. The next day I woke up with a stonking sore throat, a bad cough and runny nose. The night air had sent a chilly blast through my body, and my lack of fitness had translated it into a full-on cold. To accompany this, forty-eight hours later, I experienced soreness from hell. My legs felt like I'd pushed them to summit Mount Everest, while all I'd done was eight paltry summits in the Mournes.

I confided in my coach, complaining to him how my body had fallen apart after so little relative stress. In addition to this, my right knee hadn't felt right since my Mountain Leader assessment a few weeks before. There was a niggle in it that was not going away. Carrying around a heavy rucksack for five days while wearing chunky hiking boots hadn't done my legs any favours.

'Just rest,' Eamonn said after hearing me out. 'We'll take each day as it comes.'

I felt like burying my head in my hands, informing him that I'd never be fit or well ever again. My running days were obviously over. It's amazing how sick and injured runners can be so brilliant at melodrama.

After working with Eamonn as my coach for over six years, however, I had enough experience to know that he was probably right. His level-headed advice had always proved sound. There was no point stressing about how my body was. All I could do was rest up so I could start back training again once better.

It took well over a week before my cold cleared up enough to go back with my training plan. Then, when I began my sessions, I had to start all over again with the build-up in intensity and length. It was highly frustrating.

'You've enough strength and endurance already,' Eamonn reminded me when I cursed my fitness levels. 'You've enough to get you through this.' I had somehow forgotten that I wasn't preparing for a winter Denis Rankin Round from scratch. I had more than decade's worth of ultra mountain running already in the bag. I also had tons of experience, of knowing what to eat, what to drink, what to wear, and what to do when I'd hit an inevitable low-point. All these elements when put together meant that my fitness didn't have to be spectacular to give the round a shot.

Speaking with Paul also helped me put things in perspective.

'You said you didn't mind if you don't get home within twenty-four hours,' he reminded me. 'And sure, you've been going up and down mountains all year with your mountain-leader training and business. I'm sure that'll count for something.'

Even Edinburgh-based Jonny Muir's words about what made rounds special resonated with me even more now. It wasn't about record setting. It was about preparing, recceing and giving it a go. So what if you didn't get under the allotted time? Just the experience leading up to the day, as well as the day's journey itself, was what was ultimately meaningful.

Once I'd gotten a few more weeks of training done, I arranged to meet up with Paul to do another section of the round's route. We were still discussing about the time of the day we'd like to start, but knew that stage one would most likely be done in the dark. This section runs from Newcastle in the north out to Silent Valley in the south and typically takes five hours.

If Paul thought he was going to have a peaceful night-time mountain run, he was very much mistaken. No sooner had we started our climb through Donard Forest, than I began on a tirade that had been festering within me for a while. The mountains were working their magic on me, giving me the space to let it all out.

'Bloody banks,' I said, pushing harder with the pace than I should have so early on in the run. 'If I have to fill in another of their bloody forms, I'll feckin' scream.' In the preceding weeks, Pete's estate had officially gone nowhere. I was still pushing paper, making calls and visiting solicitors and financial institutions, all to no avail.

'Sure it's always like that when dealing with wills,' Paul reminded me, trying to keep up. 'You wouldn't believe how much hassle I had getting some prize bonds signed over from the post office once. It was a nightmare!'

'Yeah but it's nearly a year since Pete died,' I said, power-walking at speed. 'You'd think someone, somewhere would just feckin' hurry up. Their bureaucracy is killing me.'

'Look it,' Paul said. 'You've given them all the documentation they've asked for. This is out of your control now.'

I looked down at the pine-needled ground, peering through my clouded breath conjured up by head-torch beam. I didn't want to admit to Paul that he had a point. He was right that I had no power over the issues that were annoying me. I just had to forget about them and let them follow due process.

'Well I'm still pissed off,' I said, before begrudgingly shelving my rant. I could hear Paul laughing at me quietly.

We emerged from the forest to the splendour of Slieve Donard arising before us in the moonlight. Its silhouette beckoned us to go forward and climb this magnificent peak, the first one on that night's mountain menu.

I couldn't help seeing the irony of what we were doing. There was me informing parents about the dangers of going up Slieve Donard with their kids, and yet here I was in mid-November in the pitch black doing exactly what I'd advised against. If anything happened me, I'd never live it down. Fortunately I had told enough people about our route and ETA, I had packed sufficient safety equipment with me so that, if anything did go awry, we'd have been grand.

As Paul and I climbed higher and higher towards Slieve Donard's top, we encountered icy patches on the granite pathway, frozen puddles that if stepped on wrongly could cause a dangerous slip.

'Not warm out tonight,' I said, carefully minding where I put my feet. The clear night skies, which lent us perfect visibility, meant that any warmth the mountains had captured that day was being lost to the stratosphere.

'Shur, isn't that what a winter round's all about?' Paul said. I didn't mind though as, thanks to my mountain-leader training, I knew exactly the right clothes to wear. The only thing was that I was probably a little overdressed. I could feel the sweat accumulating under my multiple layers as we broke into a run on the summit's plateau. This was why we needed to do these night-time recces; to work out exactly what we needed to run in these winter conditions.

If this had been a summer round with a night-time start, the sun would rise just as we left the wall at the Bog of Donard on the climb up to the second peak, Chimney Rock. A winter round meant that we didn't have the luxury of light at this stage. Though I knew these mountains well, though I had travelled this route many times before, everything looked slightly different in the dark. Paul and I slowed to find the right path to bring us to Chimney Rock's summit.

'Not a bad night for it,' Paul said as we hit the cold cairn with our hands. We stood for a moment in the still silence, gazing over at the mountains we had left to climb. In front of us lay Rocky Mountain, then behind that the blackened outlines of Slieve Beg, Cove Mountain, Slievelamagan and Slieve Binnian. With not another soul in sight, with no trace of even a scary monster, it was an oasis of peace out there. The administration conundrums I was going through back home quietly paled into insignificance.

'Fancy a bit of sandwich,' Paul said as we jogged our way over to our next peak. Paul didn't like people crashing on him while in the mountains. He was infamous for force-feeding people who ran with him, to keep their energy levels topped-up.

'What ye got?' I said, hoping it would be palatable.

'Chicken tikka on brown soda bread,' he replied, shoving a massive hunk of sandwich wrapped in cling film under my nose. The spicy smell was enough to make my stomach lurch.

'You can seriously eat that and run straight afterwards?' I said, reaching instead for a bland cereal bar in my side pocket. Paul's masala mix would make me vomit within a couple of strides.

'Come on,' he said. 'Homemade and everything.'

'You're grand, thanks. I'll stick with my belVita.'

Such recces were a good time to test out everything that would be involved on a potential round. We weren't just checking our route finding but also our nutrition strategies. I made a mental note to keep well away from any of Paul's exotic sarnies when the day finally arrived.

We continued on after Rocky Mountain to link up with the Brandy Pad. I felt like one of those smugglers from times gone by, hurrying along this mountain path in the dead of night, even though their journeys were fraught with far more peril than our own nightly excursion.

Paul and I finally hung a left to get us on the ridge that would bring us towards Silent Valley. As we climbed, my legs felt tired though infinitely better than my outing with the fearless female five. Within a couple of weeks, my body had started to adjust to the idea of taking on a round. It was extremely heartening. I had also, in the intervening time, made a few tweaks to my GPS. Not that I even needed the device right then. The moon was shining so brightly that we could see exactly where we were headed.

'If we get a night like this on the round, we'll be sorted,' Paul said. I agreed with him. The shapes of the mountain silhouettes were more than sufficient to guide us on our way. The ground was also hard from the cold temperatures, making it quick and fast to cover. If the conditions were as good as this come the day, a winter round wouldn't be that taxing.

I had feared that the final long, steep and rocky descent from Slieve Binnian down to Silent Valley would prove treacherous at night-time. As we eased our way down it became apparent that, with good enough head-torches, it was totally manageable. The drops from various boulders on the path weren't as high as I feared, allowing our beams to safely guide us down.

The successful completion of this trial run allowed us to finally make a decision regarding our start time. With all of stage one possible in the dark, we opted for a 9.30 pm start time. It would mean that stage two, from Silent Valley to Deer's Meadow would also be completed at night time, finishing it hopefully just before dawn at 7.30 am. That would allow stages three and four to be done in daylight, before embarking on the final stage, stage five, when darkness fell again.

With a plan now in place, it was just a case of waiting for the arrival of winter and of suitable weather to allow us to attempt our round.

CHAPTER 24

WAITING

The hardest part of doing a round is turning up at the starting line. If it were an officially organised race, you'd have at least paid an entry fee. Even if you were sick, unfit or injured, you'd still feel compelled to turn up and run because of the money you had parted with. The problem rounds have is that there is no charge; they are absolutely free to do. There are zero financial implications if, leading up to your round attempt, you change your mind and back out.

The other problem with doing a round is that you can do it any day or time that suits you. Such fantastic flexibility does not work in its favour. A set race date means that you can count down to it and know, come what may, the event is taking place. With a round you can always put it off until tomorrow, next week or next year.

The mystery of why people put on the long finger these zero-cost do-whenever-you-like rounds deepened as I watched the Art O'Neill Challenge taking place in mid-January. It is a brutal event starting at midnight from Dublin's city centre, tracing the route taken by Art O'Neill, his brother Henry and Red Hugh O'Donnell on 6 January 1592 as they escaped from Dublin Castle. Journeying across wild terrain, they sought safety in Glenmalure, a valley hidden deep in the Wicklow Mountains fifty-three kilometres away from their jail. That year 800 people had applied for the 200 places available to take part in this challenge.

Though the length of the Art O'Neill is half that of a round, the often snowy conditions combined with its midnight start time means that it is still a serious undertaking. During the same period, not even one person put themselves through a winter Wicklow Round that was covering some of the exact same terrain. It appears that if it's free and you can do it any-time, no one is really that interested.

After much thought and discussion, Paul and I decided not to do a winter round exactly on Pete's anniversary. I wasn't sure how I would react to the physical exertion of undertaking a ninety-kilometre mountain run while simultaneously having the mental toll of being one year on from his death. Getting together a support crew two days after Christmas Day might have also been difficult if people were still in holiday mode.

When it came down to it, Pete's anniversary passed peacefully. I had made the decision to go away, to take a break far from the house, away from Rostrevor and anything else that could serve as a reminder. The kids didn't even click that it was happening, and their own excitement about the Christmas period helped distract me from the date's significance.

Come January, Paul and I sketched out a couple of weekends when both of us were free to do a round before the winter round date window closed at the end of February. It had to be on a weekend as opposed to mid-week if we wanted others to run with us, and with a 9.30 pm start time, that nar-rowed it down to us beginning on a Friday or Saturday evening. Which day we went ultimately depended on the weather. We had to just sit and wait to see if there was a twenty-four hour slot where conditions were relatively settled.

Despite our tentative plans, I was also starting to suffer from the prospect of actually turning up to the starting line of a winter Denis Rankin Round. Even though I'd already secured the support of other mountain runners, the idea of backing out was becoming very tempting. It was probably because I was feeling a little down around that time. It could have been a bit of January blues, when you've had enough of the dark and cold and are longing for a hint of summer light and warmth. January is always a bit of a drag.

My lack of energy could have also been due to having built myself up to getting through the firsts – the first Valentine's Day, the first birthdays, the first Christmas, the first wedding anniversary. 365 days on from Pete's death marked the end of this year of firsts, and yet, I still didn't feel all right. I suppose I had braced myself for those significant dates, and so was ready for them if they unsettled me. Come January, embarking on thirteen months since I last saw Pete, I'm not sure what I was expecting when it became a year of second-time round. Whatever it was, I had just hoped that I would feel better than I did.

Things all came to a head when Aran was invited to a school friend's birthday party, which turned out to be a trip to the local cinema with the birthday girl and all her mates to see Frozen II. With Cahal not invited but begging to go as well, I was forced to tag along with the both of them. Our movie outing was all going fine, with plenty of popcorn and sweeties to entertain us while we watched the adventures of Elsa and Anna unfurl. That was until Elsa lost her magic frozen powers, powers that had kept the adorable snowman Olaf up until then alive. Next thing I saw was Olaf slowly but surely melting away in Anna's arms. I couldn't cope. I burst into floods of tears as I watched Olaf disappear. It wasn't so much the idea of

Olaf dying that made me so emotional, but the fact that Anna was there with him, holding him tenderly throughout.

'I never got to say goodbye,' was all I could think. 'I didn't get to say goodbye to Pete.' It is a sad day whenever an innocuous Disney film can stir up such profound thoughts and feelings about your partner's suicide. I quickly scrubbed away the tears before any of the children or parents saw them. I didn't want my personal issues ruining the birthday party.

Through all these unpredictable emotions, somehow the winter Denis Rankin Round seemed like the only thing that could provide me any sort of focus; that was helping me distract me from my unease. Even if I didn't want to do it anymore, even if I thought it was a really stupid idea, even if I was still getting upset by small things in daily life, it was the only thing that seemed capable of pulling me through that horribly dreary start to the year.

As my mind oscillated between giving it a go and ditching the whole thing, the ever-persuasive orienteer Sharon Dickenson popped up on my Facebook messenger. Since my post on my club's page, she had off her own bat managed to convince and corral even more orienteers and mountain runners to support me on a round attempt.

'I've made a spreadsheet!' she announced joyfully on a day when I was feeling particularly down. Such a statement would admittedly make the stomachs of most people lurch, while for me it somehow served to perk me up. I clicked on the link to see in one column the list of the thirty-nine mountains we needed to visit together with the names of road crossings where we could pick up supplies. Beside these were columns filled with names of people who would navigate, carry gear and proverbially hold our hands on the mountains. I felt genuinely overwhelmed by their support. 'If you send through a map of the route you want to take, I can get it copied and sent out to all the main navigators,' she said. 'And then if anything needs moving around logistic-wise, I'll just update the spreadsheet.'

Up until then, I hadn't thought through the critical importance of our support team. I had considered them thus far as a 'nice to have' in terms of moral sustenance and supplies. It hadn't occurred to me that they would be people who, when I was faced with such self-doubt, would be the ones who would believe in me when I didn't have the energy to do so myself. When all I could think of was the hurt and pain that the round would involve, all Sharon could talk about was how tremendously exciting it all was. Just when I was riddled with worry and fear, Sharon and the team became my much-needed cheerleaders that I didn't even know I needed.

I had previously completed my solo summer round in twenty-one hours twenty-four minutes, my timings having been diligently recorded by a tracking device that I had carried throughout that day. Previously recorded split times at each of these summits and road crossing are usually a good guide for future support teams to know where and when to meet someone on route. With a winter round, however, I had no idea how long each leg would take me. Given the poorer weather, soggy underfoot conditions, prolonged hours of darkness and my own diminished fitness levels, it was inevitable that it would take me far longer to complete than my summer round. With the hope of completing under the twenty-four hours still alive, Sharon and I agreed to make up a twenty-two hour fifty minute schedule, just dipping under the allotted time with a bit to spare.

When I say 'made up', it was pretty much that. No other female runner had attempted a winter round, so there was no precedent to aim for. All the men who had taken on the winter challenge had opted for an early morning start as opposed to our 9.30 pm proposal. Where they would have had daylight for faster running, we'd be still trudging through darkness, and vice versa. Our plan involved a lot of guesswork, but we'd carry trackers on the day so the support team could turn up early or later depending on our online progress.

With the anchoring force of Sharon and her spreadsheet, I resolved to batter on and continue with my preparations. My night-time recce with Paul had revealed that I needed to do something about my extremities. Coming off Rocky Mountain, we had ended up on a marshy section that hadn't looked as deep as it was. Ploughing my way through it, my legs soon plunged shin deep into ice-cold water. It took a good five minutes of running for my feet to warm up again in their lightweight running shoes.

I took the time to contact UK-based ultra-runner Carol Morgan, winner of the multi-day Dragon's Back race that traverses the length of Wales, as well as two-time winner of the non-stop Spine race that Shelli Gordon had competed in. We had never met, but her Irish origins meant that I felt bold enough to reach out. If I needed some advice about how to stay warm and comfortable over a long, cold mountain run, she was the perfect person to ask. Despite her status as one of the UK's top ultra-runners, she kindly took the time to reply to my enquiry. Few are the sports where the elite are so willing to assist those who ask for their help. Carol recommended waterproof socks as well as waterproof mittens to help fend off the cold and wet. Warm hands and feet can sometimes make the difference between going the distance and giving up entirely.

I'd hoped to try out my new purchases on an early January recce of stage two with Paul. With our decision to run from Silent Valley to Deer's Meadow in the dark, we thought it was best that we went out to confirm our timing choice. I'd not run that section since May 2018 during my own summer round completion, so I wanted to remind myself of that part of the Mournes.

Unfortunately our laid-out plans came to nothing. The day before our proposed outing, snow fell. It wasn't an issue in terms of the run, as we were prepared to hit some sort of snow on the ground. The problem was the access roads to the start and finish, with the high ground at Deer's Meadow proving particularly difficult to reach.

'We'll just wing it on the day,' I said to Paul in a message calling off our plans.

'It'll be grand,' he replied. 'Sure we know where we're going already.'

I agreed with him. Paul and I knew the area well enough. Together with our GPS and our additional navigator on the day, there was enough knowledge between us to get us through that section. Ultimately, Paul and I understood we couldn't prepare for every eventuality. Something was bound to go wrong on the round, something that we were incapable of controlling, and it was just a case of having the ability to deal with whatever the issue was, as opposed to having practised everything we could think of in advance.

It was now just a question of waiting for a suitable weather window for us to give the round a go. The first slot we had earmarked was the second-last weekend in January, a date when most people happened to be free.

The weekdays running up to Friday 24 January proved remarkably good. Some lovely high pressure was sitting over the Mournes, giving us a spell of perfectly dry weather. The only problem was that the lack of wind meant the mountains were often smothered in mist, making visibility poor. The absence of cloud cover also resulted in unpleasantly cold conditions. There was no way we were going to get sunny, mild, dry and still conditions for the day. We just had to figure out what were deal breakers in terms of weather, and just go for it if on balance the conditions were okay.

I was also itching to get moving. If we didn't go the weekend of 24 January, it was an opportunity missed. We'd soon be in to February and some key people already had plans pencilled in for that month.

What forced my hand was the fact that the high pressure was forecast to leave us that Saturday afternoon. In its place, wet and windy weather was on its way, with no sign of it budging in the near future. Going back and forth between weather forecasting websites, I thought it was worth taking the risk. If we headed out on Friday evening, we might just be able to outrun the approaching storm.

I ran the idea past Paul, who was happy to go with my suggestion. I then messaged all our supporters.

'We're on,' I said. 'Let's do this.'

CHAPTER 25

DARKNESS

Petrified. That's how I felt in the days leading up to that Friday. Totally petrified.

It is a well-known fact that ignorance is bliss. I longed for such naivety. Having completed the Wicklow Round and the Denis Rankin Round already, I was well aware of how hard this winter round would be. I'd get blisters, lose toenails, get friction burns in parts of my body that were not meant to be rubbed incessantly. My stomach would turn, would refuse to take on the calories I needed to sustain my journey. My legs would scream in agony, would refuse to take another step. I'd get tired, so tired that I'd want to curl up in a ball and beg to be left out there on the mountainside. I was well aware that my mind would rebel, ordering me to give up and go home.

And yet there was a time and place when I thought this winter round seemed like a really good idea. There must have been some sound rationale behind this thought process if I was finding myself at this stage. I couldn't have trained hard for the last six months, dragged myself out on night recces, and made plans with so many people if there wasn't a point to all this.

Experience told me that this was the moment when I had to switch off my brain. There's a moment when you're on a rollercoaster, just as you reach the top of the curve when you just have to go with it and free fall.

I was on automatic pilot as I pulled my car into Donard car park that Friday evening, an hour before the off. I saw Sharon already there with other members of that evening's support team. From afar, they all looked considerably more relaxed than me. Approaching them I could hear them joking around, as if we were just meeting up for a social night out in the local pub. If only.

'Where's your gear box?' Sharon asked me, quickly getting down to business. 'Hand it over to Susan when it's ready. Susan, you know what to do.' Sharon's efficiency momentarily distracted me from the task at hand.

Susan had been one of the first victims of Sharon's enforced recruitment policy. Though she had managed to sidle out of doing a three-hour plus mountain run with us, somehow she had instead landed one of the round's most daunting jobs. Susan was tasked with sneaking into Silent Valley, the locked up reservoir under Northern Ireland Water's ownership, to meet us there at three o'clock in the morning. Susan had in turn convinced Cara, my mountain leader trainee buddy, to come along for company.

'Thanks for doing this,' I said to Susan as I deposited my gear-box at her feet.

'What? Breaking into Silent Valley at 3 am to wait for a bunch of nutters to come off Slieve Binnian? Wouldn't miss it for the world,' Susan replied. I couldn't help smiling at her sarcasm. 'Listen,' she said, her voice taking on some gravity. 'I had to ask Cara to remind me why we were doing this again. And do you know what she said?' I shook my head. 'Because we want to help a friend go for a run to remember her husband.'

It was nice to hear Cara's straight thinking. When it all boiled down to it, tonight's excursion really was as simple as that.

Paul also looked relaxed as he arrived. I was glad I had invited him along. He was such an experienced mountain runner and adventure racer, having tackled a host of difficult and daring races. He was the obvious person to have along for the next twenty-four hours.

As more and more helpers gathered, I wondered if I should do a speech of some sort, to mark the occasion. Walking towards the official start underneath the Donard Park entry arch, I realised it wasn't necessary. Everyone knew exactly why we were there. There wasn't any need for any pomp or ceremony. Actions speak louder than words, and the fact that the mountain community were right there that night for Paul and me said more than I could ever articulate.

Three other runners were there to accompany Paul and me on our first stage from Newcastle to Silent Valley. We were fortunate to have Billy Reed, the incredibly experienced orienteer and ultra-runner, as our principal navigator with me ready to act as back-up. In the lead-up to the day, Eamonn had volunteered the services of adventure racer, Shane Kenny. After Eamonn had described how strong and fast Shane was, we roped him in to carry our safety gear. I was also very happy to see the phenomenal sky runner Jackie Toal coming along for the outing. Together the five of us huddled under the arch for the parting photograph.

After so much build-up to the moment, the start felt quite surreal. We just waited around until someone's phone showed it was exactly 9.30 pm. Then with whoops and claps from our supporters, people who'd meet us that night or the following day on some random mountain roadsides, we quietly jogged away in the direction of the awaiting summits.

It was so good to finally get started after the months of agonising and anticipation. I recognised the feeling of running. The company was familiar. Even the darkness was something that I felt comfortable with after my mountain-leader wanders and recent night-time recces. I wasn't even worried by our late evening departure time. After having children, I was well used to spending a whole night awake if and when required. We were getting off to a perfect start.

As we left the forest behind and headed up the steep slope of Slieve Donard, I noticed however that my legs weren't as sprightly as I'd hoped. Billy, Jackie, Shane and Paul seemed to be all climbing far faster than me. All of sudden, my suppressed doubts came rushing to the fore.

'I'm not fit enough for this,' I thought, as a gap opened between us. Looking at my watch, I could see that it wasn't even 10.30 pm. 'If I feel this way after only an hour, how will I manage for twenty-four?'

It was at that moment that I saw Paul push up to the front of the pack. I heard a mumbling of words. Then, without me increasing my pace, I miraculously caught up with them all. It was obvious what had just happened. Paul had seen that I was struggling and had told the front guys to wait up. He knew what being at the back could do to a person's thought processes. Right then, I felt embarrassed to make the call to ask them to slow down. I needed a buddy to see what's going on, someone who was happy enough to intervene on my behalf. No matter what we're going through in life, we all need a friend like that.

Reaching the summit of Slieve Donard at 10.44 pm was a sign that, despite my reservations, we were going well. Sharon's spreadsheet had given us one hour fifteen minutes to hit the cairn, so we were officially one minute ahead of schedule. It was still very much early days however. Descending off the summit towards Chimney Rock, away from the glitz and glare of Newcastle town, it soon became apparent how really dark it was. There was no moon out that night, like the time Paul and I did our own recce. Our hope to see all the mountains strung out in a line was quickly dashed. Then to make matters worse, thick mist rolled in, mist I'd never seen the likes of in all my years of mountain travels.

Billy and I both whipped out our GPS devices as visibility plummeted. As we started our climb towards Chimney Rock, we could see less than ten metres in front of us. Even with our trusty technology, we somehow strayed from our intended line and stumbled into a boulder field that wasn't marked on our maps.

'Where's that feckin track gone?' I shouted over to Billy. Everything looked so strange. My GPS told me we were beside the path, but I literally couldn't see it. Nothing made sense.

'Over here I think,' Billy said. We clambered over to him, losing precious time. Nothing. I couldn't believe it. We hadn't even reached the second summit on our itinerary of thirty-nine, and already we were lost. Was my attempt to do a winter Denis Rankin Round going to be scuppered so soon?

'For feck's sake,' I muttered, deciding to ignore what my sense of direction was telling me to instead religiously obey my screen. After what seemed like hours, but was probably thirty seconds, the GPS informed me that I was on the path once again. I looked down and saw some faintly worn grass below my feet, mingled with a bit of mud. This was what we were meant to follow to the summit.

This brief lapse in route finding made us hyper vigilant. I also realised it wasn't fair to place the main burden of navigation on Billy. The white-out conditions we encountered were exceptionally stressful. Both of us needed to keep an eye out.

The flipside of making me pay attention to my GPS was that it stopped my needless fretting about my fitness level. My brain couldn't worry about two things simultaneously. The imperative of not getting lost instead made me focus solely on finding our way.

After finally locating Chimney Rock's cairn, we bounded down its heathered slopes, journeying west towards Rocky Mountain. The mist was so thick that it wasn't until I was within touching distance that I saw the seven-foot Mourne wall. I'd never been so glad to see it!

The advantage of the mist was that it acted like a blanket, keeping in some of the heat that would ordinarily have been lost to clear skies. All of us had layered up well before beginning, clothing that could now get stripped off in the relatively balmy winter conditions.

From Rocky Mountain, we could take a slight breather in terms of navigation. It was back to the wall, then along the unmistakable Brandy Pad before taking on the ridge running south to Silent Valley.

'So much for waiting for perfect conditions,' I said to Paul as we started our climb up Slieve Beg. There was always going to be guesswork in terms of the weather forecast.

'We got lucky alright when we did the recce,' Paul said. 'Ah well, we've started now, we might as well get on with it.'

I couldn't help thinking that at least it wasn't cold or raining or windy. Sometimes, even when things seem to have gone wrong, there's an awful lot that's still going right.

We eventually arrived into Silent Valley at 3.19 am, after nearly six hours of running. Our spreadsheet had suggested that we should have reached the reservoir at 2.59 am. Despite this delay, I knew we were lucky to get away with only losing twenty minutes given the poor visibility we had just encountered.

I was happy to see Susan and Cara's headlights shining through the dark.

'Hello, hello,' they shouted cheerfully, glad to see us too.

'That's mad up there,' I said, unclipping my bum-bag to refill it with supplies. 'You can't see a thing!' It was my excuse-cum-apology for being late and making them hang around in the pitch black for us.

'Tea, anyone?' Cara shouted, holding aloft a flask. 'Sorry it's shit, but Susan made it. She has no idea about how to make a good brew.'

While Susan set about defending her tea-making abilities, my hand shot up. The warm liquid was so good that I quickly ordered a refill and downed it in similarly fast fashion.

'Ready to go?' I asked the running team after barely two minutes had passed. The best way to make up time lost on the hills was by not hanging around at support stops. Shane looked up at me from where he had just sat down and made himself comfortable, a full Pot Noodle in his hand. He may have been a strong adventure racer, but he didn't know that getting quickly in and out of transitions is how the older, more experienced racers make up their time when competing against young ones like him. Without complaining in the slightest, he quietly set his Pot Noodle down and stood up to go.

While Jackie bowed out, Billy's daughter, Chloe, joined us on this second stage from Silent Valley to Deer's Meadow. Like her Dad, Chloe is a mountain runner and orienteer, but more importantly, she is a passionate advocate for improved mental health, particularly amongst men. Having pursued a degree in psychology and undertaken research in how to improve mental health amongst military personnel, she really wanted to join us on a section of the round, to run in solidarity with our cause.

Jogging across the top of the dam, I started to feel unwell. Up until then, I had been chomping away quite happily on food, successfully staying well away from Paul's stinky sandwich fillers. It's important to keep eating and drinking through a challenge like this so you have enough energy. But all of a sudden, I felt sick and unable to stomach anything. Experience told me however that, if I slowed, if I waited a while, my appetite would probably return.

Fortunately this paid off, and soon my stomach calmed back down. Another potential disaster averted, only for a different one to rear its ugly head. If we had thought the visibility would improve once at lower levels, we were very much mistaken. The mist sat like heavy pea soup as we journeyed through the valley, along Bann's Road towards Doan Mountain. If I had hoped to have the visibility I had the day Pete and I climbed this mountain, then I was very much mistaken.

'So, on your right, there is a lovely view over the reservoir,' I said to Shane as we hiked up the track. 'And on the left, Lough Shannagh is really pretty.'

'Lovely,' Shane replied. 'Must come back and see it for myself one day, when you can actually feckin' see something.'

'First times in the Mournes so?' I asked, to which Shane replied in the affirmative. For all he knew, we could have been bringing him up and down the same mountain all night. Only our trackers, accessible via an Internet connection that we didn't have, could prove the contrary.

I felt slightly glad as we approached Doan, the tenth mountain on our list. Normally the summit rises fiercely above the ground, trying to intimidate anyone looking to climb it from its western side, a feat we were about to attempt. With such poor visibility, all we could see instead was some heather and bog sloping upwards into the murk. It kept us focused on the present.

By now Chloe was starting to slow a little, so Billy suggested that Shane, Paul and I go on to the top, then meet them around the other side of the mountain. Navigating on my own without Billy's expert assistance, I started to second-guess where we were going. The pressure to find the right path leading to the peak was immense. I'd been up Doan many times with clients, and was well aware there were paths all over the place, leading in random directions, many of which terminated over cliffs. The area was also notorious for mountain-rescue call-outs, with people often getting lost on these slopes. After a full night of running, with nearly eight hours on my feet, I had to summon up all my powers of concentration to make sure I didn't feck this up.

The relief of finally hitting Doan's summit plateau did nothing to alleviate my stress levels. To get off this dangerous peak, I knew it was important to double back on ourselves rather than continue due east straight towards Ben Crom, the eleventh mountain on the round. Suddenly, though, I saw Shane and Paul heading straight towards Ben Crom and one of Doan's many cliffs.

'Is there a way down here?' Paul asked, peering dangerously over the edge to shine his light out over the rock. Even with a beam that shone several metres, all it illuminated was sheer darkness.

'Get back from there!' I shouted, frantic that they'd start to climb down.

Looking back on it, I can't help wondering if my mountain run was trying to imitate the trials and tribulations Pete went through while he was ill. Had Pete felt as scared as I did right there on Doan Mountain? Could he only see darkness and the prospect of a fatal fall no matter which way he turned? The difference though was Pete chose to go alone, to not confide in friends or counsellors or medics. I, however, was with my friends, and together I was convinced we could get out of this alive.

All of a sudden, my mountain leadership mode snapped in. I was responsible for Paul and Shane, and I needed to get us safely out of there.

'We need to retrace our steps,' I said. 'You've got to follow me.' Even when we came up against a seemingly impassable boulder section, I stayed true to the GPS line. Soon we were off the mountain, leaving its crags far behind.

We rounded the summit to see Chloe and Billy's head-torch lights. Billy quickly signalled that Shane, Paul and I should continue on towards Ben Crom, and that they would meet up with us on our return journey when en route to Carn Mountain. At this point I was torn. As a mountain leader, there was no way I would let a group split up like this. But we were also trying to do a winter round, something that necessitated us to keep moving. It was only because Billy was such an experienced mountain person that I agreed to go with the plan.

Paul, Shane and I thrashed our way over to Ben Crom, a trackless mountain rarely visited. The winter conditions meant the heather was low, not in full bloom like a summer round. The previous week's dry weather had also caused the ground to dry out slightly, making crossing the terrain a little less arduous. I was trying to stay focused on the positives.

Picking up Billy and Chloe on our return journey, we trudged our way back to the ever-reassuring Mourne Wall. It was now to act as our handrail to Carn Mountain, Slieve Muck and down to Deer's Meadow road crossing. With the worst of the night navigation finally over, I started to relax.

Regardless of this comfort, I knew at Deer's Meadow we'd face a stark choice. We were already twenty minutes down after stage one. We had lost a lot of time trying to get up and down Doan, and over to Ben Crom. Was it worth going on? Was it even possible to finish within twenty-four hours now that we had lost so much time? Maybe I was right; this whole winter round thing was just a really bad idea. I knew deep down no one would criticise me for giving up at this stage. At least I had given it a shot.

The only thing was, I was feeling okay. My stomach had settled. I knew where we were. My legs were tired but still moving. It was worth at least finishing the night section, getting to the next road crossing at Deer's Meadow, and making a decision there. I was a bit battered and bruised, but I had enough experience to wager I could recover and move on.

After a slip-slidey descent of Slieve Muck, we arrived at Deer's Meadow at 7.21 am. The clock showed that we were forty minutes behind, putting us on a twenty-three hour thirty minute finish if absolutely everything else for the rest of the day went exactly to plan.

Even if I wanted to stop right there, when I saw the fresh faces of our stage three runners, I just didn't have the heart to let them down. They had waited for us for nearly an hour, huddled in cars in the middle of the darkened mountains on a Saturday morning when most people were still in bed.

The main thing I clung to was, when Sharon had drawn up the split times, I had noticed that at the end of each stage she had put massive time buffers. She had assumed that we'd sit around for twenty minutes or more drinking tea, changing socks and shooting the breeze before heading off on the next section. If we could cut such breaks down to a handful of minutes, we could make up a lot of the lost time.

So leaving Billy, Shane and Chloe behind, Paul and I crossed the stile on to the slopes of Pigeon Rock Mountain, to see if things would get any better come sunrise.

CHAPTER 26

LIGHT

I remember well the day I asked Kathleen Monteverde to help me with a winter Denis Rankin Round. Kathleen had recently completed a solo round in June of that year, after coming heartbreakingly close the month before. On her first attempt, after twenty hours of running and with only three mountains to go, she had had to pull out because of palpitations and light-headedness. Broken yet undeterred, she went back out four weeks later and nailed it.

Kathleen is also one of the founding members of the Round, having known Denis Rankin personally. Though she initially thought the round was impossible, when she saw it laid out on paper, there she was at the age of fifty-six becoming the oldest female finisher.

When I told Kathleen what I wanted to do and my reasons why, her face immediately lit up.

'I would love to,' she said, her voice full of overwhelming kindness. I remember feeling a knot lodge in my throat, a wave of relief that I didn't have to try and argue my case to convince her to come along. 'I've been waiting for someone to ask me to help. It would be my pleasure,' she added.

Now there she was, fulfilling her promise, Kathleen forging to the front to lead us up Pigeon Rock Mountain. We were accompanied by her weekend running buddies, Steven Morgan, Rónán Davidson-Kernan, Sam Trotter and Pippa the dog. Though I had never met any of these people before, it was nice to see new faces. Paul of course thought this was fantastic. He always enjoys a good chat on the run. I'd run out of conversation topics and we'd already caught up on all our news. Now he had a whole bunch of new people to talk to.

I also wasn't in the mood for a natter. Even though I'd sworn to Paul that it didn't matter if our finish time was over twenty-four hours, at this point I had to admit to myself that I'd been lying. It did matter. Regardless of how much I wanted to deny my competitive self, I longed to have my name on the winter round completers' list. I wanted us to get back in line with our regimented spreadsheet schedule.

And then we got lucky. Summiting Pigeon Rock, the dawn arrived and with it we could see a couple of extra metres. And then all of a sudden, the mist vanished. The Western Mournes we were journeying into are notorious for attracting fog. The haze's disappearance was close to a miracle. Finally we could see the Mournes in all their moody majesty. The morning sun lit up the ground's yellow and brown winter cloak with gentle tinges of orange. It was stunning.

Words cannot capture that feeling of moving from night to day, to have the seemingly endless blackness around you retreat to allow you to finally see. Maybe this is why the Darkness into Light movement is so powerful; because it provides so many with the hope that the light of self-care, community and acceptance can replace the darkness of stigma, self-harm and suicide.

Putting away our head-torches, we started to move, faster and faster, making up the time we had lost during the night. Heading over to Wee

Slievemoughan, I was even treated to one of Kathleen's homemade biscuits. Thanks to finding a sheep track through the knee-height heather over to Windy Gap, I could actually concentrate on enjoying her baking as opposed to minding where I put my feet.

It would have been nice to chat more with Kathleen on that stage, but she was far too busy with her map and compass. She was taking her job very seriously and couldn't be disturbed. She was right, though, as the desolate stretch from Shanlieve to Finlieve through towering peat hags and lunar-like rock beds required fine navigation. The time flew by, as before I knew it we were heading towards Slievemeen, the twenty-first mountain on the round and the furthest south we would get that day. Though one of the least known mountains in the Mournes, it is by far my favourite. Its unrivalled views over Carlingford Lough and the rugged Cooley Mountains make it a hidden gem.

The joy of turning around and beginning our journey north again was only superseded by our time. Somehow, Kathleen and her team had played such a blinder that we had recouped most of the minutes we had lost during our ten hours of darkness. Arriving at the handover at Slieve Martin, we were only seven minutes behind. They had done a fantastic job.

They placed us in the safe hands of our next set of runners, Geoff Smyth and Denise Mathers. Denise had joined me for that first night recce I'd done with the fearless five females. I hate being late, so was glad not to have kept them waiting too long.

As I sat down to prepare my bumbag for the next stage, I saw fellow orienteer Jonny O'Hare standing there spectating with his two kids. It was good of him to come all the way up the hillside to cheer us on. His children were the same age as mine; four and six years old respectively. They were firm friends with my kids, as well as bitter orienteering adversaries. Jonny's kids couldn't quite understand where Aran and Cahal were in this melee. They had never seen me without them in tow.

'Give Moire one of your jaffa cakes,' Jonny said to his six-year-old daughter Aoife, pushing her in my direction. I looked up at her from the ground, to see the disappointment in her face at the suggestion of sharing them. She held out the packet extremely reluctantly.

'You're very good, but you have them,' I said with a smile. I had so much other junk food in my bag that I could easily forgo a jaffa cake. Aoife skipped away, exceedingly happy that I hadn't depleted her limited supply.

Paul and I were good to go within a couple of minutes. This stage, the fourth out of five, was notorious for being the roughest in terms of terrain. This was the section that, come what may, we had to do in daylight. We both braced ourselves for what was to come.

Denise and Geoff were raring to go. Having a team with fresh legs served as a great morale booster. Soon we were running towards Crenville, the nemesis of all Denis Rankin Rounders. No event on the race calendar attempts to go near this summit, with good reason. It is surrounded by waist-height matted grass and ankle-tangling tussocks, which mask boo-by-trapped bog holes beneath. You can barely walk, let alone run. It's more of a case of trip, stumble and fall towards its summit.

Having touched the wooden stakes at the top, Denise then set about doing an emergency evacuation from the place. The joy of rounds is finding the best routes between summits. Both Paul and I on our own previous rounds had managed to extract ourselves from Crenville via a very long and tiring journey to the west. Through her own perseverance and numerous recces, Denise had found a much better way.

'Follow me,' she said, bounding off in a northerly direction, the rest of us giving chase.

Within a couple of minutes, we had popped out on the main forest track with not a mound of grass or tussock in sight.

'Now that was seriously clever,' I said. 'We'll have to name that route after you.'

'Ah sure, it was nothing really,' Denise replied. 'Just got lucky finding it.'

It was obvious we had made up some time via Denise's spectacular short-cut. I wasn't entirely sure how much, however, as when I looked down at my watch, the screen was blank. Its battery designed to last for up to a day had, after years of use, been whittled down to half that.

I, like many runners, am addicted to my watch. Knowing how long I've run, how far I've gone, what heart rate I'm on gives me a sense of control over my exercise. Now that my watch was dead, I expected annoyance to set in. How was I going to know how much time we had left? Much to my surprise, however, I just undid its clasp and placed the watch carefully in my bag. As long as we kept moving like we were doing, I figured we'd be fine.

Putting my watch away, not having the constant data updates, proved hugely therapeutic. For the first time that day I started to relax. After feeling so petrified in the lead up to the round, I hadn't anticipated that I'd actually enjoy any part of it.

'Show me the way to go home!' Paul started to belt out as we jogged along the track past Red Bog after summiting Slievemeel. It may have taken him fourteen hours, but he had also run out of things to say. He was now resorting to singing to pass the time. 'Join in with me,' he shouted. Geoff, Denise and I briefly humoured him.

With the Denis Rankin Round being such a hard challenge, you'd assume that you're not meant to have any craic. You're supposed to be sweating, sleep-deprived, exhausted, in pain. The challenge is meant to be gruelling and overwhelming. But, in the company of other amazing mountain runners, in the midst of such stunning mountains, I started to really enjoy our day out in the Mournes. Even the weather was playing ball. It wasn't too hot, too cold or too windy. The mild conditions were hanging around long enough to give us a settled day.

As we started the climb up Cock Mountain, the round's twenty-eighth mountain, I went to take out my empty bottle to refill it from Rowan Tree River. The Mournes' streams are full of clean mountain water, so I was more than happy to drink from them.

'Sure give it here,' Geoff said, 'I've mineral water in my bag.'

I didn't want to refuse his kind offer, seeing that he had lugged a two-litre container of RiverRock around in his rucksack on our behalf for the last two and a half hours. What he handed me back was a thing of beauty. I could see right through my bottle, the water totally transparent compared to the bog-tinged liquid I would have extracted from the mountainside.

'Oh my goodness,' I said, taking a swing. 'There's no sand in it.'

I had to laugh at myself, hearing how something so simple could give me such pleasure. There was me, happy enough hydrating with brown, murky mountain water only to receive crystal-clear, grit-free water to drink.

If my life at the time of Pete's death had felt like a glass quarter-filled, then maybe the main reason I had coped thus far was because my expectations had slowly changed. One year on, I was glad I still had a glass. I felt fortunate that there was still something left inside it, that my boys and I were alive and well.

Maybe I had also changed a little since Pete's death. Perhaps I had

replaced my glass with something a little smaller, one with fewer expectations, making the milk I had come further up its sides. With contentment
with smaller things, with gratitude for what I had as opposed to what I
didn't, it meant that I could keep going with life. It was like having an
espresso cup filled to the brim, as opposed to a ten-ounce coffee mug that
contained a mere trickle.

Jogging off Slievenamiskan, the final peak that we'd summit with
Geoff and Denise, my legs were going well. My coach Eamonn was right.
Regardless of what I believed myself, I did have enough endurance to get
me through this task. Even my knee niggle was behaving itself, an unexpected bonus.

Dipping down to Spelga Dam, the final road support stop before the
end, we had somehow made up even more time. No longer seven minutes
behind like at the last checkpoint, we were beating the spreadsheet's predictions by an incredible forty-two minutes. It was a great buffer to have.

Even though we arrived early, our support team were already there, waiting for us. The wind had started to pick up as predicted, and they were
being blasted by its gusts that gathered speed as they skimmed over the
surface of the unobstructed reservoir.

It was great to see our head spreadsheet-operator Sharon there together
with a host of other faces. Ciarán McAleenan, David Bell, Stephen Bickerstaff and Niall Gibney were bouncing around, trying to keep warm as
they waited for Paul and I to refuel and replenish our supplies. I didn't
know these guys at all, another a bunch of amazing mountain runners that
Sharon had managed to round up on our behalf. It was humbling to think
they had given up their Saturday afternoon to come run with us. Our head
navigator for this final section, Niall Gibney had completed his own winter

Denis Rankin Round a mere seven weeks beforehand, but was still ready and willing to help me out on mine. People can be really amazing sometimes, a fact that is easily forgotten.

By now I was starting to feel the effects of over seventeen hours of running. I guessed we had at least five hours more to go. Scurrying into the tent that Liam Smyth from the mountain-rescue team had kindly constructed, I refocused, ate, drank, put on dry layers, popped some painkillers and got back out there to finish the final ten peaks.

As forecast, the weather soon started to close in. By 4 pm, cold winds started to blast across the mountaintops. The only reprieve was the fact that it was blowing from the south, and as we journeyed north, I hoped it would push us home. We had also re-joined the Mourne Wall that lent a modicum of shelter, something we would follow for the next couple of hours.

With time still ticking, I was well aware that we had left the biggest climbs to last, Meelbeg, Meelmore, Bearnagh and Commedagh, four of the largest in the range. It was a daunting final run. So I caught up with Paul and said it as clearly as I could, 'I want to go home.' The tone in my voice said it all. I wasn't going to pretend that I was doing okay, that I was loving it all now. I was starting to feel broken and I needed help.

Maybe this is a lesson Pete could have learned, but never had a chance to; by acknowledging how you really feel, messy or damning as it can be, help can be found. I've had the good fortune to learn this lesson, thanks in part to the counselling I had. I've also learned, from spending time in the outdoors, to acknowledge and voice my feelings. I know if I don't say something when I'm struggling, there can be serious consequences.

On hearing this, Stephen took my bumbag and then simply stayed by my side. He didn't talk; he was just a comforting presence that made my spirits pick up. Sometimes that is all that's necessary, not a grand gesture, just to know someone is there, to right you if you stumble.

I felt even better when we reached Hare's Gap just as it got dark. With my watch out of action, I had to gauge how we were going by what the sun was doing. I remembered the original plan was that sunset was meant to be on Meelmore, a place we had passed an hour earlier.

Even though we were ahead of schedule, I wasn't sure if my head was right. I could see someone waiting for us at the col, but still couldn't trust my eyes. It turned out this figure was Liam from Mountain Rescue, the person who had lent us his tent at Spelga Dam. The only issue was, despite it being the end of January, even though I was wearing four layers on top and just about keeping out the cold, Liam was standing there in shorts. I was convinced I was hallucinating, something that often happens during sleep-deprived ultra runs. It later transpired that I had been right; he was dressed for sunny weather. Mountain rescuers are obviously made of hardy stuff.

With nightfall at Hare's Gap, it was time to pause and take out head-torches. Grabbing mine out of my bumbag I stood beside Liam to put it on. Only that, when I looked at it, my brain was too tired to work out which bit went where. With my impaired mental functions, it looked remarkably like a tangled-up G-string.

'Can you help me with this?' I said to Liam, starring at the jumble of straps in my hand. He obviously didn't see the G-string as, with one quick flip and as if by magic, it retook its form as a fully functioning head-torch.

The weather refused to let up as we continued to tick off Slievenaglogh and Slieve Corragh. It pummelled us, extracting the last vestiges of energy that Paul and I had. Grasping on to the Mourne wall we were following, on to its dependable several million-year-old granite rocks, I clawed my way up the final climb to Slieve Commedagh. The wall's solid presence was a kind reminder there is often something to hold on to, if only you reach out.

There's nothing like seeing the bright lights of civilisation as you come off that final hill. Newcastle soon appeared below us as we emerged from the mist with our support team. Even better was the bright light of Mark Stephen's head-torch coming towards us, shining in the direction we needed to go. There is nothing like a crack orienteer, one of Northern Ireland's finest, turning up at just the right time on a mountain that many stray on.

We sped off the final remnants of bog and heather, picking up another orienteer Richard Gamble, before entering Donard forest. My body was tired, but my spirits buoyed knowing that we were nearly at the finish.

'What was your summer round time?' Paul asked me as we emerged from the trees.

'I don't know,' I said, my brain slow to recall such a figure. 'Something like twenty-one hours twenty-four.'

'Well, you've two minutes to beat it,' Paul said after a glance at his watch. I didn't need any further encouragement to leg it.

We booted through the car park, past the boy racers, past Sharon ringing a cowbell. Hitting the stone arch of Donard Park, we arrived safely back to the place we had started at 9.30 pm the previous night. We had completed the circuit in under twenty-four hours, the first time a woman had completed a winter round in Ireland.

'What time did we do?' I asked, once I had caught my breath.

'Twenty-one hours, twenty-four minutes,' someone replied. In cold, wet, blustery winter weather, in over eleven hours of darkness, I had managed to do the exact same time as the round I had done in the summer, in nice warm and well-lit conditions. The only difference was, this time, I had not done it alone. This time, this achievement was only made possible thanks to the incredible love and support I had received from the mountain community.

But regardless of the time, what we did together as a mountain fellowship that day was far more significant. It showed the importance of friendship, with people like Paul selflessly helping me grieve in a way that we both understood. It illustrated the strength of community, of how mountain-running friends and strangers came together to help remember Pete, even though most of them never had the good fortune to meet Pete while he was alive.

The mountains have taught me so much and have been my solace for many years. Indeed the mountains have often shown me how fragile and vulnerable I actually am, how I sometimes need the help of others so I can journey safely through them. It is this knowledge that gives me the strength to continue on, come what may.

And in the midst of this mental-health crisis that we find ourselves in, it reminds us that it is the simple things that can help us – it is being there for others, being grateful for what we have, doing things that we love. And sometimes it's just about getting out there ourselves and going for a simple run.

WHAT I'VE LEARNED ABOUT GRIEF

Grief is horrible. Losing anyone you love is heartbreaking. Even harder is when that person dies young or unexpectedly. And nothing is worse than when it appears that person made that decision themselves to end their own lives.

When I told others of my plans to write this book, they asked me to include some advice based on what I'd lived through. The problem with giving a list of dos and don'ts is that there are so many exceptions to the rule. I remember being told that the road ahead after Pete's sudden death would be 'so hard'. When it came from a medical professional, I took it differently from when given the same message by someone who was still suffering from their own bereavement and was probably projecting their own pain. I also received this message differently when told it mere days after Pete's death compared to when it was said after a year had passed. In other words, the exact same advice could help or hinder me depending on when I was given it and by whom. This is what makes giving advice on what 'works' so very difficult.

So please take this list of helpful advice with a pinch of salt. If even one rings true, then try it, and if it doesn't work, ditch it. Ultimately everyone has to find their own way to deal with their own grief suffered by losing a unique person in their lives. The important thing is trying to move forward, with kindness towards yourself and the one you loved.

FOR THOSE EXPERIENCING GRIEF

In cases of death by suicide, remember it's not your fault. Even if you replay events in your head, ultimately the decision to take their own life was theirs and no one else's. Don't blame yourself.

Make sure you sleep, especially in those initial days. It was the only thing that kept me sane. If sleeping pills are needed, take them.

Make no major decisions for the first year. Let the dust slowly settle before making any serious changes in your life.

Focus on what's important. Knowing that I had to be functioning for my two boys, and that I had to look after myself to do that, was enough of a focus to keep me going. Find something that forces you to get out of bed.

Say yes to everything at the beginning. If someone offers to mind the kids, say yes. If they invite you for a coffee, say yes. You'll soon work out when to say no.

Think about what your loved one would have wanted. More than likely, they just wanted the pain to end. Probably they thought you'd be better off without them. They didn't want you to suffer anymore. Regardless of how wrong their decision-making was, think about what they would like now. Do they want you to sit around and cry forever, or do they want you to get on with living the life they couldn't have?

If you've kids, don't lie, but measure out the truth accordingly. They might not need to know all the details, but don't make things up. You'll be surprised how well they can cope and process the situation.

Don't stop talking about the deceased or having their photos around. Remembering the good times with them might cause teary moments, but it's worse if you deny that they ever happened.

The wound from your loss is there whether you like it or not. The question is; do you want it to get infected and fester forever? Or do you want to do what it takes to make it heal and leave a permanent scar that showed how much you loved? Counselling can often help the healing process without criticism or judgment.

Look after yourself. Do something you love. Being in the mountains helped me, but you need to find for yourselves that special thing that makes you feel better.

Be with those who love and support you. They mightn't be the people you expected to be there, but that's okay.

Be part of the solution. Be okay to talk about the consequences of poor mental health, and let everyone know it's okay not to be okay.

THOSE TRYING TO HELP THOSE WHO ARE GRIEVING

Be proactive. Telling those who are grieving to 'let you know if they need anything' is comforting, but those suffering from grief don't often have the energy to reach out. Being fed was hugely helpful, so cook or shop for them. Friends who were solicitors and accountants, who assisted me with the administration side of Pete's departure, were life-savers. When I needed to set up my business, having friends walk me through the process was invaluable. Do what you do best to help, and don't wait to be asked.

Go to the funeral if you can. The bereaved then know you know the story, and don't need to explain the next time they see you.

Don't be afraid to tell them you're sorry for their loss. You mightn't want to bring up their loved one's death, but whether they like it or not, they are more than likely thinking about them that day.

Write down your memories of the loved one and send it to their family. You mightn't believe it, but funny stories are often the ones most appreciated.

Ask them 'How are you *today?*' That helps narrow it down for them, and lets those who are grieving talk if today has proved bad, or might even give them permission to share if today was actually okay.

Make no assumptions. Don't assume it's hard. Don't assume what the saddest part is. Just be there, listen and never judge someone's grief journey.

The loss of a loved one sets you on a different life path. Just make sure that path journeys through and towards something you love, and that you line it with people who love and support you come what may.

ACKNOWLEDGEMENTS

Courage is contagious[1]. This book and all it contains would not have been possible without the courage of others holding me, helping me, being at the end of the phone for me when grief was doing its worst. It is their courage that has allowed me to write down what happened, which will hopefully allow someone else to be courageous in the face of similar tragedy or loss.

I'd firstly like to profoundly thank the Rostrevor community who have been there for me throughout all of this, in particular Wiola and Se Gorman, Leona Farrell, Julie and Martin McGinn, Henry and Liz McLaughlin, Didi and the Baxter family, Teresa Parr, Aislinn Campbell, Gill Toal, Teresa Parr, Momin Malik, Paddy Byrne, as well as the teachers at St Bronagh's Primary School, Little Folk Playgroup and Seaview Nursery. Thanks too to Kellie Cunningham and the staff at the Newry Leisure Centre, Killian Byrne of Mud Monkeys, Rónán McGibbon of 1st Dromore Newry Scouts and Eiméar Kane from Inertia Gymnastics who have been there throughout for my boys.

The best way to help those who are grieving is to, 'Show up. Listen. Don't fix.'[2] To those who tirelessly showed up for me, listened to me, and didn't try to fix me, I'll be forever indebted, particularly Nathalie Houben, Suzanna Gaynor, Hilary Jenkinson, Mel Spath, Izzy Kidney, Tim Seltzer, Avril Mahon-Roberts, Breda Gahan, Brian Williams and Sharon Swan-

1. Billy Graham
2. *Refuge in Grief*

ton. I'm also extremely grateful to the PIPS team, particular Roisin Martin.

I'll be forever indebted to the mountain-running and orienteering community who were there for me, not just for the winter Denis Rankin Round, but for many mountain miles, particularly Paul Mahon, Sharon Dickenson, Susan Lambe, Juls Hanvey, Paulette Thomson, Stephanie Pruzina, Ciara Largey, members of Lagan Valley Orienteers, Shane Kenny, Billy and Chloe Reed, Jackie Toal, Kathleen Monteverde, Steven Morgan, Rónán Davidson-Kernan, Sam Trotter, Pippa the dog, Denise Mathers, Geoff Smyth, Niall Gibney, Ciarán McAleenan, David Bell, Stephen Bickerstaff, Mark Stephens, Richard Gamble, Liam Smyth, Judith Robinson, Paul O'Callaghan, Jonny O'Hare, Ian Bailey and Áine McNeill. There are not enough words to thank my coach Eamonn Tilley who has been there through thick and thin. Special thanks too to Eoin Keith, Fiona Meade, Paul Tierney and Shelli Gordon who kindly told me their stories and allowed me to share them here.

My deepest gratitude to those who walked with me on my Mountain Leader journey, in particular Rachy Sinnamon, Cara Lavery, Caris McKnight, Paul Nolan, Carol Morgan, Keri Wallace, Stuart Smith, Laura Watson and John Shiels. To everyone who has come along and supported Happy Out Adventures, especially Marion O'Hare and Anna McLaughlin, my original Parents up Peaks. I've enjoyed every one of our mountain trips.

Special thanks to Ray Jordan, Jim Hynes, Will Galvin, Ken Madden, Paddy McGuinness, Tanmay Chetan and Borann Kea for intervening when I didn't even know I needed help and for being the best friends and colleagues that Pete could have ever had. Thanks also to Helen and Nic I'Anson, Max Draper, Davide de Beni, Mueni Mutunga, Ronan Caffrey and Alice Nkoroi for reaching out so thoughtfully and keeping in touch.

To the original Derry Girls, the wonderful Cara McLoughlin, Sarah McGarry, Niamh Gilfeather, Sinead Harkin, Catherine Haddock, Adele Kane, Jane Carton and Julie Ferry. I am so glad we reconnected.

I think best in ink, so I'd like to thank Helen Carr and the team at O'Brien Press for working so tirelessly to publish this memoir. I would also like to thank Ita O'Driscoll and Kay Farrell for all their encouragement, as well as fellow authors, Juliet McGrattan and Jonny Muir, who have been part of my journey ever since *Mud, Sweat and Tears*, and who continue to inspire me to write. Special thanks too to Louise Heraghty, Catherine McIntosh, Shauna Flynn and Caoimhe Connor who encouraged me to stand up and tell my story.

I am forever indebted to those who searched and found Pete, in particular the Mourne Mountain Rescue Team including Martin McMullan and Alwynne Shannon. I would like to thank the police for their professionalism, courtesy and compassion throughout.

To everyone who wrote letters to Aran and Cahal and expressed so beautifully who their daddy was, thank you on their behalf. I hope this book will allow them to one day understand what happened and help them grow up to be resilient, empathetic and inspirational men.